I Classici del Calcio

20 Grea Gam

By Giancarlo Rinaldi

Giancarlo Rinaldi was the founder and editor of the UK's best-known Italian football fanzine of the early 1990s, Rigore!. He also co-authored a guide to Serie A with Ray Della Pietra and wrote the local history books From the Serchio to the Solway and Great Dumfries Stories. For 20 years he contributed to Football Italia magazine and later Soccer Italia and Soccer 360 and previously published the first edition of 20 Great Italian Games. He lives in Dumfries with his wife, Anne, and two children, Mia and Luca. A lifelong fan of Fiorentina he still has foolish dreams that he will see them win a third Scudetto. If Twitter is your thing, you can harangue him there under his username @ginkers.

All rights reserved – © Giancarlo Rinaldi 2015

Cover image: Courtesy JDT Sport. Design: Marco Rinaldi.

To Martino – Uno di Noi.

Contents

Introduction

When the first edition of 20 Great Italian Games came out it was really something of an experiment. I was genuinely unsure if anyone would want to read it and, even if they did, whether they would be prepared to pay for the pleasure. I quickly got my answer, however, when it turned out there was enough interest to send it – however briefly – to the top of the sports book bestseller list on Amazon. It was one of the proudest moments of my football writing life.

A lot of people said a lot of nice things about the book which was very much appreciated and a huge boost to this author's confidence. It is one thing to scribble down your thoughts for personal purposes but quite another to find there are others who have enjoyed reading them. It puts a little fuel in the tank and gets you ready for another journey along the publishing highway.

There were criticisms, too, most of them very constructive – thankfully – and I have tried to take them on board in this second edition. Team line-ups have been included this time around in the hope that they will make the tales of these memorable matches a little easier to decipher. For those who love their formations – I have used the line-ups as they appeared in the papers of the day. Most of the older games are in the traditional 2-3-5 format while the more modern line-ups are in systems more familiar to the present-day football fan. Goalscorers are also listed in the hope of increasing the clarity for those who might dip in and out of the book or read a chunk of chapters at a time.

I have also listened to the readers too, I hope, in allowing them to vote in one match for inclusion in this edition. It seemed like a nice reward for those who have put up with me imposing my ideas of what might constitute a great game upon them for the past few years via my blog and in my books. There were plenty of good nominations and they may well form the backbone of a third edition if and when I get around to writing it. In the end, it was a pulsating Roma versus Inter game from 1999 which was served up by Zdenek Zeman and Roy Hodgson which won the day. I hope you enjoy my attempt to do justice to such an incredible game.

It was my aim to get even more under the skin of the matches contained in this book in order to give anyone who never saw them the first time around a real feel of what the game was like. Or, for those who do remember, maybe it will rekindle the good (or bad) emotions which the action inspired at the time.

There should be something for everyone in these pages. All of Serie A's biggest sides are covered as well as many of its lesser lights. A wide range of different eras have been included too and the names of some great players should leap out from these stories just as they did when they were occupying the front cover of La Gazzetta dello Sport.

If you have not read the first edition, maybe this one might inspire you to do so. I like to think of it as a bluffers' guide to the history of the Italian game. Some of the most essential clashes in Calcio's colourful past are included here.

So sit back, pour yourself a nice glass of Tuscan red (or whatever your favourite tipple might be) and take a little sip of nostalgia. Serie A has gone through some tough times recently so it is nice to remember happier times or big matches which helped to establish its global reputation. It can be infuriating and frustrating, controversial and chaotic but it is very rarely boring. I can only dream that I have done it justice with this selection of 20 more memorable matches.

Giancarlo Rinaldi, Dumfries, January 2015

Juventus v Fiorentina
Stadio delle Alpi, 4 December 1994

If the match had been a meal, then that goal was its grappa moment. A searing, stinging conclusion to help digest what had gone before. And, depending on your colours, it left either a brutish burning sensation or a gentle afterglow.

Everything about the game seems, now, like a prelude to such an exquisite finish. But although it was part digestivo for an epic encounter stuffed full of goals, it was also part aperitivo to a sumptuous career to come. An Aperol-infused taster of the delicious strikes which would light up the playing days of Alessandro Del Piero.

But let's go back and set the table first before we get to the liqueurs. It was December 1994 and Fiorentina and Juventus were set to resume hostilities after a year's ceasefire due to the Viola's relegation to Serie B. Claudio Ranieri's side had already shown they were smarter than the average newly-promoted side. On the opposite bench, Marcello Lippi was charged with fulfilling the Bianconeri's habitual fixation - securing the Scudetto. It had been, in *La Vecchia Signora's* terms, nine long years since the last one.

The Turin giants were not, however, top of the table by the time the season's 12th round of matches fell to be played. That honour went to Parma with a slender, single-point advantage over Gianluca Vialli and company. Fiorentina were just a point back in third. A game which really needs no spicing up had an extra dash of peperoncino that year.

There were notable absences for both sides - much more so for the Bianconeri. The visitors were without ex-Roma man Fabrizio Di Mauro but the home team's missing list was lengthy. For one reason or another Roberto Baggio, Didier Deschamps, Angelo Di Livio, Luca Fusi, Antonio Conte and Jurgen Kohler all had to skip the match. Makeshift would be a bit of an understatement.

For all their lack of familiarity, Juve enjoyed the best of the opening exchanges before the Florentines began to flourish. The catalyst for the goal that broke the deadlock could be no other. It was, of course, Gabriel

Omar Batistuta - who had scored in each of the opening 11 weeks of the season.

This time, unusually, he did not find the net but his defence-splitting run spread panic in the Juve ranks. Angelo Peruzzi spread himself well to smother the Argentinian's initial shot but he could do nothing about the rapacious follow-up. Francesco "Boom Boom" Baiano swept the ball home with 24 minutes on the clock.

If there was incredulity at that moment then spectators would be downright dumbstruck 11 minutes later. Midfielder Angelo Carbone scampered onto a long through ball and did not think twice before thumping a shot over Peruzzi. The boys of the *Onda d'Urto* who had made the trip to Piedmont were in ecstasy. It would not last.

But it took everything Juve could muster to find a foothold in the game and it stubbornly refused to come until 17 minutes from full-time. Vialli met a cross from old White Feather, Fabrizio Ravanelli, with a bullet header and the speed with which he wrestled the ball free from Francesco Toldo's grasp suggested he believed a comeback was possible. It was his 100th Serie A goal.

Number 101 was not long in coming. The ball rattled around in the penalty box and Vialli swivelled sharply to draw his side level. Lippi puffed on a big cigar and seemed to transmit a confidence that he knew the win was there for the taking.

It came a few minutes from time with the match's iconic moment. Alessandro Orlando hit a seemingly hopeful ball forward from left back which came dropping towards earth just inside the penalty box over Alberto Malusci's shoulder. Del Piero anticipated that trajectory to perfection and - with the outside of the boot - invented a finish which left Toldo no chance. The young Juventino fell flat on his back in amazement and delight at what he had just achieved.

"This was an emotional and beautiful game, the boys showed great character to come back," said Lippi afterwards. "We did not deserve to be 2-0 down at half-time."

"It was a tough game, I'm destroyed," added Vialli. "It was hard from both a physical and a mental point of view. But I'm going through a good spell and everything is going right. I hope it continues both for myself and for the team."

Ranieri, for his part, was understandably dejected.

"We knew at the end of the first half we had the second half to play," he said with an uncanny knack for stating the obvious. "We played well in the first half and they did in the second. They got a goal back and after that they could not be contained."

The win did not allow Juve to overtake Parma at the top, that would happen a week later with another epic triumph - 4-3 away to Lazio. They lost their lead a week later but reclaimed it in the following round of matches never to look back. The Scudetto ultimately arrived with 10 points to spare.

As for the Viola, their season never quite recovered. They slithered down the table to 10th place, a long way off the positions their early form had suggested. There was the consolation of Batigol finishing the campaign as top scorer with 26 strikes but it was a meagre one.

And the boy Del Piero? He went on to be a bit of a player for club and country stacking up honours like the layers on a slice of lasagne. A swansong in Sydney the closing chapter in a glittering career. And yet he scored few, if any, which were better than that magnificent strike which downed Fiorentina nearly two decades ago. And Juventini probably still raise an after-dinner glass or two in its honour to this day.

Juventus: Peruzzi; Ferrara, Carrera, Porrini, Orlando; Torricelli (53 Tacchinardi), Paulo Sousa, Marocchi (73 Jarni); Vialli, Del Piero, Ravanelli.

Fiorentina: Toldo; Carnasciali, Marcio Santos, Malusci, Pioli; Cois (90 Flachi), Carbone, Robbiati; Rui Costa; Batistuta, Baiano (71 Amerini).

Goals: 24 Baiano, 36 Carbone, 72 & 76 Vialli, 88 Del Piero.

Verona v Milan

Stadio Marcantonio Bentegodi, 20 May 1973

There are very few grounds in Italy where those red and black devils from Milan fear to tread - but the Stadio Marcantonio Bentegodi may just be one. The reason can be traced back to a Sunday more than 40 years ago which started out as a road trip to clinch the star assigned for a 10th Serie A title but ended up in torture fit for Dante's Inferno. And it is all encapsulated in a two-word turn of phrase which has become part of the Calcio lexicon.

Fatal Verona.

The 1972/73 season had been a gruelling one for the Rossoneri but it looked destined to end in glory. They came into the final round of games with a single point advantage over chasing Juventus and Lazio. A victory against their Veronese opponents - who had already secured Serie A survival - would guarantee the title. Even a draw could win the Scudetto or, at the very least, a play-off game. In a league which springs few surprises in its closing weeks, it looked like Nereo Rocco's men had cause for confidence.

Certainly, their supporters were ready to party. They streamed across the north of Italy to cheer their heroes on to glory. But there were a couple of significant obstacles to overcome.

"We were exhausted," Gianni Rivera told Guerin Sportivo magazine recently. "The Wednesday before we had won our second Cup Winners' Cup (against Leeds United) all we needed was a bit of rest."

For their part, Hellas promised not to make things easy for the Rossoneri. Although they had nothing left to fight for from their own point of view, they promised to scrap for at least a draw. Italian football, however, is full of such hollow vows and before the game it was estimated about 30,000 Milanisti would make the trip to the Veneto to support their team. But manager Giancarlo Cadè seemed sincere in his promise not to make this what his opposite number Rocco described as "like the last stage of the Giro d'Italia, where nothing ever happens."

"I think Rocco was wrong to say that," said the Gialloblu boss. "I've got players who don't want to lose. Nobody at Verona intends to stand by like a spectator when the last stage of the Giro passes."

Cadè, in truth, had a bit of previous when it came to managing stubborn end-of-season sides. It was his Mantova team which defeated Inter at the end of the 1966/67 campaign to play a part in handing the Scudetto to Juventus on the final day of the season. Among his players that day, a certain young goalkeeper named Dino Zoff.

"That was a different situation to the one we face this Sunday," insisted the Verona coach. "That Inter side was at the end of an era and appeared to be struggling. This Milan team could be about to start a winning cycle by beating us and they don't seem in trouble at all."

But one problem which did face the Rossoneri was that their opponents possessed one of the most mercurial and madcap footballers of the day. Gianfranco Zigoni was in his first season towards becoming a hero for Hellas. "I dreamed of dying on the field in a Verona strip," he once said. "I could see the headlines - and a petition to change the stadium name in my honour."

He was the kind of talent who could win or lose a match single-handedly. Unfortunately for Milan, he took it into his head to have one of his inspirational days.

"Coming out onto the pitch, the stadium was all red and black," he recalled. "Roberto Mazzanti was running beside me and he asked me if we were in the San Siro. I felt a bit rebellious, the Gialloblu flags were there, but I think they were hidden. I said to him: 'Today we won't lose, they will have me to deal with.'"

He and his Verona team were good to his word. They took the lead before the midway point of the first half through Paolo Sirena, courtesy of some lovely Zigoni build-up work. A Giuseppe Sabadini own goal doubled the home team's advantage a few minutes later and, before a half hour had passed, Livio Luppi made it three. The Milanese giants were stunned and their thousands of fans felt a sickening sense of dread.

A Roberto Rosato strike reduced the gap before half-time but the players were still shell-shocked. The only good news for them was that Roma were producing a similar surprise in the capital and led Juventus 1-0. Long-shots for the league, Lazio, were locked in a stalemate with Napoli. The Rossoneri tried to rouse themselves during the interval.

"In the dressing room we realised we could be losing a championship in that game which meant nothing to Verona," said Luciano Chiarugi, scorer of the winner against Leeds. "We still thought we could do it, but it was a terrible blow."

There would be no dramatic comeback, however. Instead, Luppi extended Verona's lead and another own goal - this time from Maurizio Turone - made it five. In the meantime, Juventus had equalised in Rome through Jose Altafini.

Yet despite the crushing defeat, Milan still had hope. If results stayed as they were there would be a play-off game with the Bianconeri in store. But even that glimmer of light would be extinguished in the closing stages of an epic afternoon.

There was time for the Rossoneri to pull a couple of goals back - with Sabadini scoring at the right end and a strike from future Scudetto-winning Napoli coach Albertino Bigon. In between times, however, came the news which sealed Milan's fate. Antonello Cuccureddu had hit home a belter for Juventus to give them the title. At the final whistle, realising the full scale of the sporting disaster, players and fans alike were distraught.

"There were people crying and in the dressing room we didn't even have the strength to speak," recalled Chiarugi. "We didn't speak for half an hour - we were destroyed by this event. We had the star within our grasp - but we couldn't make it shine."

Rocco himself was livid, having pushed for the match to be postponed for a few days to allow his players to recover from their European exertions. He felt the heavy pitch combined with tiredness had taken its toll.

"I wanted the game put back three days," said the Milan legend. "It was, after all, a Cup Winners' Cup final, which was a prestigious target and required some effort and a fair bit of energy. And then on Sunday we were playing for the Italian championship, not my local league. Unfortunately they did not oblige and so we went into the game not in the best condition."

The 10th title, then, would have to wait until 1979. There was only some small consolation that season with a Coppa Italia victory over title-winning Juve.

Curiously enough, the Bentegodi would prove a deadly venue for Milan many years later. Locked in a battle for the 1989/90 title with Napoli, they were beaten 2-1 by Verona to effectively hand the Scudetto to the Partenopei. Little wonder Rossoneri followers of a certain vintage still shiver when they take the A4 motorway across the north of Italy to head to Hellas and back.

Verona: Pizzaballa; Nanni (34 Cozzi), Sirena; Busatta, Batistoni, Mascalaito; Bergamaschi, Mazzanti, Luppi, Mascetti, Zigoni.

Milan: Vecchi; Sabadini, Zignoli; Anquiletti, Turone, Rosato; Sogliano, Benetti, Bigon, Rivera, Chiarugi.

Goals: 18 Sirena, 27 Sabadini (og), 30 & 70 Luppi, 35 Rosato, 78 Turone (og), 83 Sabadini, 90 Bigon.

Fiorentina v Inter

Stadio Artemio Franchi, 26 November 1995

This time, it was personal. I was a man on a mission, my goal to see Gabriel Omar Batistuta score for Fiorentina. Of course, he did not let me down.

It was November 1995 and the Viola were one of a bunch of sides trying to keep pace with league-leading Milan and Parma. It was Roy Hodgson's Inter who were coming to town but they were sitting in a pretty miserable midtable position. The Florentines were in the unusual condition of being narrow favourites for the match.

I had flown out from Scotland for a double-header at the Artemio Franchi. The Milanese giants at the weekend, followed by a midweek Coppa Italia quarter-final first leg with Palermo. All I asked for a pre-Christmas treat was to see my hero get among the goals.

They were cold days with winter closing in and I was booked in a little pensione in the heart of Florence rather than taking the commute from the family home in Garfagnana. At nights I dined in fixed-price menu trattorias, people-watching and trying to blend in. I was never awkward and picky enough with the waiting staff, however, to pass myself off as a true Italian.

But my little mini-carafes of local wine gave a glorious afterglow. Could life get any better than this? Two games in the space of a few days, good food and the attractions of the Renaissance city at my disposal. Now it was time for Batigol to deliver.

I watched the Inter game on a Football Italia ticket. Channel 4's coverage was in its pomp and they were screening the match and happy to put my name on the list for press passes. It produced the traditional pantomime it almost always does.

"Rinaldi?", I asked at the ticket window and was met with a blank response. "Football Italia?", I suggested and got a similar look. "Giancarlo?", I tried, optimistically, but still without any joy. Luckily, each question prompted a cursory flip through the accreditation envelopes. I spotted one with what looked like "Channel 4" scribbled on it and pounced. "Eccolo!", I trumpeted with as much confidence as I could and snatched the prize before too many questions were asked.

Paul Elliott was on pundit duty that day with James Richardson - in a little corner of the press section tucked away under the very roof of the Stadio Artemio Franchi. I kept hoping Jimbo would ask for my expert input, but my starring role never happened. The closest I got was a call from my uncle saying he had seen my back on a live satellite stream he was picking up on his monster rotating dish back home in Scotland. I brushed with fame at last.

My recollections of the actual match are sketchy. I do recall Fiorentina slipping behind to a delightful lob from Maurizio Ganz, living up to the banner Inter fans regularly unfurled in his honour declaring, in dialect, *"El segna semper lu!"* (He always scores!). It was a statement they quickly shelved when he transferred to Milan a couple of seasons later.

The Nerazzurri had the better of that opening period. Paul Ince was patrolling the midfield to some effect and Benito Carbone linking up well with Ganz in the attack. And, of course, there was Javier Zanetti doing his usual impeccable job of bridging the gap between the defence and the forward line. They were a decent side.

And they should really have gone two ahead but Marco Branca had a shot cleared off the line by Pasquale Padalino. It was a let-off for Claudio Ranieri's men and one which they took advantage of. In the second half, they stepped on the gas and Inter fizzled out. There was only one possible outcome.

I remember (or am I fooling myself?) a feeling of expectation and anticipation rippling through the whole stadium. It was not a question of "if" Batistuta would score, it was more a matter of "when". We awaited, ready to explode when the moment arose. He teased us until about midway through the second half.

It was at that point that the slender figure of Spadino Robbiati sliced through the visiting defence on the left flank leaving Lo Zio, Beppe Bergomi, trailing in his wake. He clipped a perfect back post ball to where the Florentine avenger was waiting. He rose at the perfect moment and powered a header back across Gianluca Pagliuca's goal which he had no prospect of saving.

Grazie Batigol.

It could have felt like a long journey without that strike but, instead, I went back to my pensione with my head still buzzing with how he had lit up a dark winter's day. The streets of Florence were pulsing too with excitement for a team which was sitting at the top end of Serie A and still in the hunt for the Coppa Italia too.

I got my second helping of Bati magic a few days later. Palermo - stuck in Serie B but performing well in the cup - were the visitors. The Argentina great won and converted a penalty to give the Viola a slender first leg advantage to take to Sicily. It was enough to take them through and on to eventually lift the cup - beating Atalanta over two legs. It sparked crazy scenes of celebration in Florence with a first trophy in more than 20 years. I felt I had played my own little part with my pilgrimage to see a goalscoring hero in action.

Fiorentina finished fourth in the league that year as Milan were crowned champions. Inter were seventh and qualified for the UEFA Cup. Batigol ended up a few goals shy of the top scorer's crown which was shared by Lazio's Beppe Signori and Bari's Igor Protti - who I once met at Fiumicino airport in Rome, but that is a story for another time. Inter's top scorer for the season was Branca with 17 strikes for the Nerazzurri that league campaign.

That was all too many years ago. Since those games were played, the Viola have been through relegations, promotions, scandal and Champions League football. Batigol has long since hung up his boots. It sometimes seems to me that the Franchi rocks a little less raucously these days. And yet, if you pour me a carafe of wine and let me take a sip and close my eyes I swear I can still hear that song.

"Corri alla bandierina, bomber della Fiorentina!".

Fiorentina: Toldo; Carnasciali, Amoruso, Padalino, Serena; Piacentini, Rui Costa, Schwarz, Cois (82 Robbiati); Batistuta, Baiano.

Inter: Pagliuca; Bergomi, Festa, Paganin, Roberto Carlos (51 Pedroni); Zanetti, Ince, Fresi (76 Manicone), Carbone (83 Bianchi); Ganz, Branca

Goals: 18 Ganz, 67 Batistuta.

Torino v Juventus

Stadio Comunale, 27 March 1983

In a long and glorious career which brought about every honour in the game, Dino Zoff has few regrets. But one of his hardest defeats to take was a Turin derby which his legendary Juventus side lost in the blinking of an eye. Needless to say, it is a match which has entered Granata folklore.

Back in the spring of 1983 - as so often in the history of Italian football - there was no team tougher than the Bianconeri. Their core was formed by a huge chunk of the Azzurri side which had won the World Cup in Spain a year earlier. And to top it off they had superstars like the exquisite Michel Platini and that Polish purveyor of searing pace, Zibi Boniek.

With six games left in the campaign La Vecchia Signora was still harbouring hopes of yet another Scudetto as she was within striking distance of league-leading Roma. But her city rivals were breathing down her neck with European football on their mind. There is no such thing as an inconsequential Derby della Mole, but this one packed a punch more powerful than Primo Carnera.

It was the 127th encounter between the two sides with the old Stadio Comunale a riot of noise and fireworks. It was a Toro home game and their fans had faith in their youthful favourites. The wind would be knocked out of them by a defensive blunder within the first 15 minutes.

Operating along the Platini-Boniek axis, Juve sliced their cousins open on the left flank. However, it looked like the danger had passed when an innocuous ball from the former Widzew Lodz forward fell to the feet of Michel van de Korput. However, the Dutchman dallied and then played a suicide ball towards Giuliano Terraneo in the home goal. It was like dropping your wallet in front of an expert pickpocket and Paolo Rossi duly nipped in to open the scoring.

Eugenio Bersellini's men were struggling to get a foothold and they trudged off at half-time like a team finding it impossible to figure out a way to break their opponents down. "We gifted them a goal so we'll try to get it back in the second half," said influential midfielder Beppe Dossena.

"All our tactics have gone out the window now, but we'll try to win this game."

If they did come out with greater resolve it melted away midway through the second half. This time it was Roberto Bettega who sent Boniek clear to spread panic in the Toro rearguard. Skipper Renato Zaccarelli lunged in as the forward cut back inside the box and even the home support could not dispute the penalty award.

Le Roi stepped up to take it but, for once, proved fallible. He appeared a little too nonchalant in his approach and Terraneo was able to make a sprawling save. Much good it did him, however, as the Frenchman was quick to make amends for his error and reacted swiftly to scoop home the rebound and extend Juve's lead.

"We conceded a second goal and that put us in enormous trouble," recalled Zaccarelli. "With the quality of the team you were up against, you had to feel a bit discouraged."

"To come from two goals behind against that Juve team was practically impossible," echoed Terraneo. "Unless something out of the ordinary happens."

And then, incredibly, it did.

First a Roberto Galbiati cross was met by Dossena to give the trailing team a little hope. Then Paolo Beruatto was the provider as Alessandro Bonesso nodded home. Finally, van de Korput made amends for his earlier bungle by crossing in a ball which was thumped home with a lovely volley by the appropriately-monickered Fortunato Torrisi. Incredibly, less than four minutes had passed between the first Torino goal and the last.

"It was like taking a first punch in the boxing ring," explained Juve defender Sergio Brio. "You are stunned and then you are knocked out by the second punch. That was the classic knockout blow."

"It happened so quickly that you asked yourself - what just happened?" admitted Zaccarelli. "But a characteristic of Toro is never to give up."

Dossena, one of the goal heroes, claimed his coach had forecast the turnaround. "During the week Bersellini told us that Juve usually slow up in the second half," he explained. "So he tried to dose out our efforts. The plan was to keep them under control in the first half and increase our effort gradually during the second. That's what we did, and it worked out."

"Three goals in five minutes is unheard of," raged Juve supremo Giampiero Boniperti. "They must have forgotten that last year we came from two goals behind to beat Torino, which shows you have to concentrate all the way through the derby. Anyone listening on the radio must have thought the commentator had made a mistake because Juve, with the players we have and the experience they have got, can't get sliced apart by Toro like that."

The defensive dissection they had suffered proved fatal to Juve's title dream. They tried to recover from the stunning defeat but had to accept second place behind Nils Liedholm's Giallorossi. It was to be the precursor to a disappointing end to the campaign as Giovanni Trapattoni's men went on to lose the European Cup Final to Hamburg. A comeback triumph in the two-legged Coppa Italia final with Verona (they lost the away leg 2-0 but won the return 3-0 in extra time) would provide some consolation.

As for the victors, they had clearly given their all. In the five remaining games of the season they gathered just a single point and finished in eighth place, well short of Europe. It might not have been the conclusion they had hoped for but few fans were overly concerned. They were still too busy checking in disbelief that the events they witnessed on their home ground against their most bitter rivals had actually taken place.

Torino: Terraneo; Van de Korput, Beruatto; Zaccarelli, Danova, Galbiati; Torrisi (78 Corradini), Dossena, Selvaggi, Hernandez, Borghi (59 Bonesso)

Juventus: Zoff; Gentile, Cabrini; Bonini, Brio, Scirea; Bettega, Tardelli, Rossi, Platini, Boniek.

Goals: 15 Rossi, 65 Platini, 71 Dossena, 72 Bonesso, 74 Torrisi.

Roma v Inter

Stadio Olimpico, 3 May 1999

In any league in the world it would have been something out of the ordinary but in Italy it was almost extraterrestrial. But when Zdenek Zeman is around you can always expect the unexpected. With the attacking power at Inter's disposal, it produced a game which skyrocketed from the opening exchanges and never returned to earth.

The first goal was a masterclass in two players doing what they did best. With characteristic vision, Roberto Baggio slotted a beautiful ball through the heart of a Roma defence which looked more flaky than extra mature Parmesan. At his peak, and even when he went beyond it, there was no way you could give Ronaldo that kind of space and the Brazilian bomber was on to the ball like a shot. Poor old Michael Konsel in the Giallorossi goal might have been asked to play as a sweeper but he was floundering around like a toddler trying out his water wings. The Nerazzurri striker rounded him with ease and rolled the ball into the net. It was but an appetiser for what was to come.

A few minutes later and the Divin Codino was sprinkling more creative magic over the game. When a lovely outside-of-the-boot pass from Javier Zanetti found him free on the right wing he had all the time and composure in the world to pick out Ivan Zamorano. The Chilean striker appeared to mishit his shot a little but it looped past Konsel just the same to extend the visitors' lead. A little thumbs up from Roy Hodgson, sitting on the Inter bench alongside Giacinto Facchetti, was the only sign of excitement from the English coach.

It was maybe just as well he was pretty unflappable for there were plenty of emotional twists and turns in store. The next one would reopen the match as a clear tug on Paulo Sergio produced a penalty for the home side. It was converted, low and to the goalkeeper's right, with typical composure by Francesco Totti. Three goals were on the board and the game was less than half an hour old.

But this Roma team had not exhausted its reserves of generosity and it opened up its defence once more to a searing Zanetti run. Another sweet through ball appeared to have pushed Zamorano a little wide but he had clearly got a taste for goal. This time there was no doubt about his intentions as he sweetly chipped the hapless goalie to once again give the Nerazzurri a two-goal buffer which they would retain until half-time.

The Giallorossi, however, came out of the traps flying in the second half. It was Gianluca Pagliuca's turn to get caught in no man's land when he was tempted off his line by a neat chipped ball from Damiano Tommasi. Paulo Sergio beat the goalkeeper to it and nodded over his half-hearted attempt to intervene. Once more, the final outcome of the match was in the balance.

Things would only get more intense just a few moments later when Paulo Sergio turned provider and swept in a cross from the right wing which Marco Delvecchio soared to meet and guide past Pagliuca with his head. If the home team were showing all sorts of shortcomings at the back, they were more than making up for it in attack. The hallmarks of their coach were there for the world to see.

And they only continued when, a little before the hour mark, Inter broke from defence once more. It looked as if the home defence had managed to break up the move but a tackle fell to the Nerazzurri midfield and Zamorano was sent galloping clear. He showed a cool head and a healthy dose of altruism to roll the ball into the path of Ronaldo rather than seek his own hat-trick. The Brazilian duly dispatched his shot into the back of the net. Once more the Milanese outfit had the lead.

They would hold onto it for more than 20 minutes before getting caught once more by a move which combined slick skills and good fortune in equal measure. A backheel from Paulo Sergio sent Eusebio Di Francesco dashing clear on the left. He played the ball to Delvecchio in the Inter penalty box who rolled the ball back to Paulo Sergio. His attempted shot was so woeful that it turned into a cross for Totti who nodded the ball back into the path of Di Francesco. The midfielder swept the ball home to make it 4-4.

There were chances at either end for Youri Djorkaeff and Delvecchio before Ronaldo had a sweet finish from a pinpoint Baggio cross ruled out for a very close offside call. Most spectators thought that might be the end of the dramatic events in the Stadio Olimpico. But the footballing fates had one last little trick to perform.

It would be Baggio who once more provided the ammunition for his team-mates to gun down the home side. A lovely free-kick picked out the advancing Diego Simeone and he powered home the header which would decide the game. El Cholo's celebrations seemed to show that he was as bemused as anyone by the events which had just taken place.

"It was just 90 minutes but it felt like two days," admitted a flabbergasted Hodgson. "I wasn't expecting a game like that, I always expect a goalless draw. Nine goals in a game are unusual anywhere, never mind in Italy.

"It is clear that as well as the quality of the attacking play all these goals are down to defensive errors too," he added. "I am going to watch the video of this game during the week to try to sort things out at the back and I'm sure my friend Zdenek will do the same. Roma played well and the way the game panned out we could just as easily have lost. Luckily for me, Zamorano, Baggio and Ronaldo saved us."

It was not the catalyst for the end-of-season rush into the European places that Inter might have hoped for. They lost back-to-back games with Parma and Venezia which meant a final day triumph over Bologna was only enough to give them eighth place. Roma finished three places better and went into the UEFA Cup. They both ended up with two of the worst defensive records in the division which showed their springtime clash in the Stadio Olimpico was more or less typical of their crazy campaigns.

Roma: Konsel; Quadrini, Zago, Aldair, Candela; Alenichev (32 Tommasi), Di Biagio (84 Tomic), Di Francesco; Paulo Sergio (79 Gautieri), Delvecchio, Totti.

Inter: Pagliuca (63 Frey); Simic, Bergomi, Colonnese, Silvestre; Zanetti, Simeone, Cauet; Baggio; Zamorano (79 Djorkaeff), Ronaldo.

Goals: Ronaldo 17 & 56, Zamorano 22 & 35, Totti 26 pen, Paulo Sergio 47, Delvecchio 49, Di Francesco 79, Simeone 87.

Milan v Napoli

Stadio Giuseppe Meazza, 13 April 1986

It was a game which would become, in the space of a few years, a Scudetto classic. But, back in April 1986, the teams involved were still under construction. What magnificent edifices Diego Maradona's Napoli and Silvio Berlusconi's Milan would ultimately become.

This springtime clash was one of the first games for the Rossoneri under new ownership. The media mogul had only just taken over the club from the debt-ridden reign of Giuseppe Farina. He had promised to build them into the greatest side in the world but, in the meantime, he brought dancing girls, a marching band and a Formula One racing car as part of the pre-match entertainment.

Napoli, for their part, looked a lot more like the finished article. Three points clear of their opponents in third place they were, nonetheless, a fair distance adrift of Juventus and Roma who were locked in a tussle for the title. Still, the Azzurri travelled to the San Siro with a justifiable degree of confidence.

That would only be boosted by a total emergency in the home defence. Franco Baresi and Mauro Tassotti were both suspended while Filippo Galli was ruled out with injury. It meant ex-Roma legend Agostino Di Bartolomei was expected to play as a makeshift sweeper to try to shore up the back line.

"The game with Napoli will be decisive to keep us in line for a UEFA Cup place," said Rossonero boss and former playing hero Nils Liedholm. "It is not a position I would have expected us to be in at the start of the season but we must try to keep a hold of it.

"But if we miss out I could not criticise my players because they have already had an amazing season," he added.

One man particularly under pressure was goalkeeper Giuliano Terraneo, whose errors had been blamed for recent defeats by Inter and Roma. There was also talk, which proved to be true, that he would move on at the end of the season.

"My mistakes against Roma and Inter were not decisive," he insisted. "I just had some uncertainty and I take responsibility for that. But at my age (he was 32 at the time), I don't think I have to prove anything to anyone."

The squad selection emergency prompted Liedholm to go for all out attack with a team featuring Mark Hateley, Paolo Rossi, Pietro Virdis and future San Marino international Marco Macina. The midfield was patrolled by Ray Wilkins, giving a distinctly English accent to the side. It proved to be an imbalanced formation which Napoli quickly swept aside.

Ottavio Bianchi already had the backbone of what would be a team which would win the title the following year. Maradona pulled the strings and ended up "enchanting" the San Siro with his play. Liedholm's plans to try to play on the attack were in tatters after less than half an hour.

Bruno Giordano was first off the mark. He sped through a motorway up the middle of the Milan defence to roll the ball past Terraneo. The space being afforded the Napoli attackers was a major concern to the home support.

Then it was time for a bit of Diego magic. Faced with a pack of Milan defenders on the edge of the box he produced a little shimmy to work a bit of space. Then, with minimum backlift, he stabbed a shot between them and past the sprawling Rossoneri goalkeeper. It would have been goal-of-a-lifetime stuff for many, but for Maradona it was run-of-the-mill.

It was enough to persuade Liedholm that his tactical efforts had failed and he made a switch before half time. Macina was sacrificed to let jobbing defender Carmelo Mancuso try to shore things up at the back. It worked, to some extent at least, and Milan had two shouts for a penalty - one for a tug on Hateley, another for handball - before half-time.

In the second half, the visitors appeared to relax a bit too much and the home side finally put Claudio Garella in the Napoli goal to the test. He was found wanting from a low-drive of a free-kick on the hour mark struck by Di Bartolomei. He may have seen the ball late but his howls at his defenders suggested he knew he could have done better and was trying to shift the blame.

The netminder more than made up for it after that, mind you. A string of fine saves ensured Napoli came away with a precious win in the San Siro – a feat it would take them more than 25 years to repeat. They would finish an impressive third at the end of the season while the Rossoneri folded to seventh and out of the European spots.

"We got things wrong at the start when we were piled up in the opposition box," said Liedholm. "I sent four forwards out but they were supposed to take turns to work back into midfield but Napoli got the lead before we had time to sort things out. That, for me, is why we lost but I don't think we deserved to - they shot twice and scored twice, while we created at least ten good chances."

"There were three penalties for us," lamented Hateley. "But the referee gave none of them. That is football I guess, even if we did miss a few chances when we didn't take advantage of good passes."

As for Diego, he was beaming post-match. "I said we would win in San Siro," he purred. "This success crowns our season which sees us finish third and in the UEFA zone. We have achieved the club's goals. Now to aim for the Scudetto, we need to strengthen the squad."

He was to get his wish, more or less. Fernando De Napoli and Andrea Carnevale brought the salto di qualità - leap of quality - needed to secure the league title - and Coppa Italia - the following year. In the process, Maradona's revered status in the city was secured. Not that it was ever in much doubt.

As for the Rossoneri, there was a revolution on the horizon. Arrigo Sacchi and the Dutch masters were set to arrive soon and transform their fortunes from midtable strugglers to probably the greatest team on the planet. And that would produce some epic clashes with the boys from the San Paolo in the years to come. For much of the late 1980s and early 1990s, their encounters in Campania and Lombardy were some of the most memorable matches in the European game.

Milan: Terraneo; Icardi, Maldini; Russo, Di Bartolomei, Evani; Macina (38 Mancuso), Wilkins, Hateley, Rossi, Virdis.

Napoli: Garella; Bruscolotti, Marino; Bagni, Ferrario, Renica; Bertoni (88 Caffarelli), Pecci, Giordano, Maradona, Filardi (53 Celestini).

Goals: 12 Giordano, 23 Maradona, 60 Di Bartolomei.

Roma v Sampdoria

Stadio Olimpico, 22 September 1996

Recent years have seen Sampdoria's stock fall and rise again in dramatic fashion to fuel dreams of recapturing their glorious past. For the Blucerchiati have been star turns in some memorable episodes of Italian football both domestically and in Europe. One of their more epic performances was delivered by Vincenzo Montella about 20 years ago – when he helped to destroy a club he would later serve both as player and manager.

It was just the third round of the 1996/97 campaign when the Doriani made the trip to Rome to face a Giallorosso side sitting joint top of the table with Paul Ince's Inter and, more surprisingly perhaps, an Igor Kolyvanov-inspired Bologna. Sven Goran Eriksson was in charge of a Genoese outfit still constructed around the classic skills of Roberto Mancini. His opposite number, Argentinian Carlos Bianchi, could count on an all-South American strike force of Abel Balbo and Daniel Fonseca.

The visitors came with a 4-3-3 formation that put Mancio at the heart of the attack with lesser and more youthful lights like Marco Carparelli and Vincenzo Jacopino beside him. Juan Sebastian Veron ran the midfield flanked by Frenchmen Christian Karembeu and Pierre Laigle. In defence, disciplinary nightmare David Balleri and former Milan legend Alberigo Evani provided forward impetus from full-back roles. Moreno Mannini and Sinisa Mihajlovic stood guard in front of Fabrizio Ferron in goal.

Roma responded with a 4-4-2 designed to provide a solid platform for their Argentinian and Uruguayan hitmen. Swedish midfield organiser Jonas Thern was supported by Francesco Statuto, Damiano Tommasi and Amedeo Carboni. The defensive line included the elegance of Brazilian Aldair and the more rough-house Enrico Annoni. Former Samp man Marco Lanna and disastrous Argentine import Roberto Trotta completed the line shielding goalkeeper Giorgio Sterchele.

The game would turn out to be an initially tense one, locked at 0-0 until nine minutes into the second half when a defensive error let the Giallorossi take the lead. An overly-nonchalant Mihajlovic lost possession near his own goal and Balbo was quick to pounce before any other Doria defenders could close him down. It prompted the move which would swing the match.

Sensing he needed to turn the tide quickly, Eriksson removed Veron and sent out Montella. Having already been forced to replace Laigle with Marco Franceschetti in the first half, he only had one substitute left at his disposal. He used it before the hour mark to bring on old-stager Giovanni Invernizzi to replace an ineffectual Carparelli. It was a huge gamble but one which paid off in minutes and in some style.

There was more than a little good fortune in Samp's 65th minute equaliser. A run started by Karembeu saw Montella play the ball into the path of Mancini. His shot was blocked by Sterchele but rebounded off Aldair to trickle into the home side's goal.

Bianchi's response, having already replaced Statuto with the more attacking Francesco Moriero, was to imbalance his team even further by putting Martin Dahlin into the fray for Tommasi. "I had to go for the win," insisted the Roma boss after the game. But it backfired on him disastrously.

Mancini flourished in the space left behind the Giallorosso defence and pulled away on the left flank in the 74th minute before driving towards the bye-line. He then cut back a perfect low cross to Montella who happily passed the ball into the roof of the net. The Little Aeroplane set off in a celebration that would give Romanisti a lot of pleasure in years to come, but not in this particular encounter.

Two minutes from time, Mancio delivered the coup de grace and in trademark style. He again broke clear on the left and evaded a despairing dive from Sterchele to round the goalkeeper. He then made it look the simplest of things to curl home a shot from a narrow, narrow angle. The future Manchester City boss was a player with skills very few in the Italian game have ever been blessed with.

He helped to complete the rout in injury time from the same flank. A low, driven shot was parried straight to the feet of Montella who was only too happy to tap another goal home. Roma's disastrous capitulation was complete and the knives were already out for their manager.

"The dream is already over!" blasted the Corriere Della Sera just three weeks into the season. "The little Roma of last season is back – wasteful up front with Fonseca who messes up the easiest of chances and calamitous at the back with defensive lapses caused by inexplicable spells of taking the foot off the gas."

"Sampdoria were clinical," insisted Bianchi. "We had a couple of chances to kill the game after Balbo's goal and we missed them. They took all the opportunities that came their way. But that is football, nothing comes easily."

"I don't think Roma played badly," he insisted. "Before we went ahead we had two or three chances to take the lead. But I don't think there was such a big gap between the two sides."

One man at the centre of the fans' displeasure was Trotta, a part of Bianchi's Velez Sarsfield side which had won the Copa Libertadores a couple of years before. He hit back at a perception that he was a manager's favourite who was not up to Serie A standards.

"When we lose, everyone whistles me," grumbled Trotta afterwards. "That hurts me. I am not this club's saviour, the team wins or loses as a group. I am here to play for Roma, not for Bianchi."

History, however, would show that he would not play much for the Giallorossi and end up cited as one of the biggest Bidoni – disastrous overseas players – of the last 20 years. His manager did not fare much better, being shown the door in springtime as Roma struggled near the bottom end of the table. They would end the campaign with just 41 points – a mere four points above relegated sides like Cagliari and Perugia.

Sampdoria would finish in sixth place that campaign with far and away the best attack in Italy and qualification for the UEFA Cup secured. Montella alone struck 22 times in Serie A (finishing second in the capocannoniere race to a young Atalanta forward called Filippo Inzaghi) and Mancini grabbed 15 himself. They were one of the most prolific attacking partnerships ever seen in the famous hooped shirts. Anyone wearing the shirts these days has a lot to live up to.

Roma: Sterchele; Annoni, Trotta, Aldair, Lanna; Tommasi (75 Dahlin), Statuto (67 Moriero), Thern, Carbone; Balbo, Fonseca.

Sampdoria: Ferron; Balleri, Mannini, Mihajlovic, Evani; Karembeu, Veron (54 Montella), Laigle (15 Franceschetti); Jacopino, Mancini, Carparelli (59 Invernizzi).

Goals: 53 Balbo, 69 Aldair (og), 77 Montella, 87 Mancini, 90 Montella.

Napoli v Juventus

Stadio della Liberazione, 20 April 1958

When Juve come to town, you take whatever vantage point you can. In spring 1958 in Naples, they packed behind the goals and onto the balconies of properties overlooking the stadium to get a glimpse of the all-conquering Bianconeri. In the hope, of course, of bringing them down a peg or two.

These were the days when John Charles and Omar Sivori - perhaps the oddest couple in Calcio history - were at the peak of their powers. The tall, powerful and scrupulously fair Welshman and his more diminutive, skilful and sneaky Argentinian colleague were on their way to amassing 50 league goals between them. But at the old stadium in the Vomero district – they would move to the San Paolo the following season - they still harboured hopes of a home victory.

The reason for Neapolitan optimism was quite simple - they had a pretty decent team of their own. Not, perhaps, on the level of La Vecchia Signora, but a quality outfit nonetheless. And, moreover, they had already defeated the Turin giants on their own turf - the only team to have achieved such a result in Serie A that campaign.

They had a goal machine of their own in the shape of Brazilian Luis Vinicio. Dubbed 'O lione - the Lion - by his home support he tormented defenders the length and breadth of Italy. He would have a field day against a Bianconero defence which was still a long way from the impenetrable unit that Giovanni Trapattoni would oversee in the 1970s.

The title was already pretty much in the bag for Juve when they travelled south for the clash on 20 April. Ten points clear with six games left to play under the old two points for a win system was an almost unassailable lead. Still, the Partenopei - their nearest rivals along with Padova - hoped to at least delay the Scudetto celebrations.

Those ingredients produced a classic mix. Vinicio opened the scoring as early as the fourth minute. Some good build-up work on the right allowed him to control the ball easily and slam it past visiting netminder Carlo Mattrel. It was the start of a deluge of goals.

The Bianconeri's response was just a couple of minutes in coming. A seemingly innocuous cross from the right was knocked towards goal by Charles and caused a panic in the home defence. An Elia Greco deflection saw the ball end up in his own net to level the match.

But the huge crowd was not going to settle for a share of the spoils and howled their favourites forward. Some neat interplay saw winger Luigi Brugola break clear of the Juventus defence. Once again, it was a pretty straightforward task for him to nip the ball under the diving goalkeeper.

Vinicio should have stretched that lead early in the second half when he was put clean through on goal but this time Mattrel was quick off his line to deny him. It gave The Old Lady a lifeline she was quick to grab. Gino Stacchini cut in from the right and hammered home a shot from a tight angle to make it 2-2 after less than an hour's play.

That gave the visitors greater impetus and they tested the home goalkeeper Ottavio Bugatti a couple of times as they pushed for the win. But it would be Napoli who struck next with just 13 minutes left on the clock. Future Scudetto-winning coach with Fiorentina Bruno Pesaola got away on the left and his cross found Vinicio at the back post. He made amends for his earlier error with a sweet finish into the top corner.

It looked like being the winner until a free-kick in the 86th minute was floated into the box by Boniperti. It appeared the Napoli defence had cleared the danger but, instead, Antonio Montico cracked in a shot through a crowd of players which gave Bugatti no chance. It was back to the drawing board for Amedeo Amedei's side.

But, just like their manager, they had goals in their blood and would send their fans home in delight. Another poor defensive clearance dropped to midfielder Gino Bertucco and he had no hesitation in driving the ball home. The supporters piled up behind the goal went crazy. The final whistle brought a full-scale pitch invasion.

"The most exciting game of the season," announced old Italy boss Vittorio Pozzo in his match report of the day. "The championship has not been mathematically decided as many expected it to be. The team which rose to its feet and stopped that happening - in a most determined and surprising manner - was Napoli. Juve did not get their own way because they found somebody able to outplay them. It was, as they say, an explosive match."

"Napoli played this game as if it were a matter of life and death," he concluded. "They gave their all. They deserved their success not because they were technically superior nor for any refined tactics but essentially for the effort, enthusiasm and commitment they threw into the fight. And it meant Juve's title victory had to be put off for the time being."

"We were unlucky," said a disappointed and disgruntled Juventus president Umberto Agnelli. "The final result came about a bit by chance. The last goal, the one which decided the game from Bertucco, came as a result of a free-kick which should not have been given."

It would only prove to be a minor bump for the boys in black and white on their road towards the Scudetto. They won it with eight points to spare over second-placed Fiorentina. As for the Partenopei, the win did not send them towards the runners-up spot they had hoped for. They managed just one win in their last five fixtures (against Inter) and suffered a couple of heavy hammerings - 7-0 by Udinese and 4-0 at Vicenza - to finish a still-respectable fourth. But one of the undoubted highlights of their campaign was producing one of the best matches of the year when Serie A's biggest name came visiting.

Napoli: Bugatti; Greco, Posio; Morin, Franchini, Beltrandi; Di Giacomo, Bertucco, Vinicio, Pesaola, Brugola.

Juventus: Mattrel; Boldi, Garzena; Corradi, Montico, Emoli; Stacchini, Boniperti, Charles, Sivori, Stivanello.

Goals: 4 Vinicio, 6 Greco (og), 24 Brugola, 58 Stacchini, 77 Vinicio, 86 Montico, 88 Bertucco.

Fiorentina v Milan

Stadio Giuseppe Meazza, 25 August 1996

There may never have been a more pure explosion of joy from a Fiorentina player or for fans of the Viola. Gabriel Omar Batistuta has just smacked a raking free-kick into the top corner of Sebastiano Rossi's goal to effectively clinch the Italian Super Cup for the Tuscan side against Milan in the San Siro. He wheels away in delight looking for a television camera into which he bellows his love for his wife Irina. The word ecstasy was rarely better used.

That late summer night in 1996 was one of the pinnacle moments for that Batigol-inspired side. There was also the Coppa Italia win a few months earlier, some fine Champions League nights and a Scudetto dream under Giovanni Trapattoni that collapsed when injury cut down their talismanic Argentinian. Still, the Supercoppa will live long in the memory.

Regardless of the trinket-like nature of the trophy, this was no ordinary Milan side. The Rossoneri had just stomped their way to a 15th Scudetto under Fabio Capello sweeping all before them. He had moved on to Real Madrid to be replaced by Oscar Tabarez, but the home side remained overwhelming favourites. They put out three quarters of their most famous defensive line with Paolo Maldini, Franco Baresi and Billy Costacurta strung across the back. Only Michael Reiziger at right-back hinted at the change of guard.

The rest of the side was not half bad either. Marcel Desailly, Zvoni Boban, Dejan Savicevic and George Weah were the foreign stars while Demetrio Albertini and Marco Simone completed the team. Edgar Davids was a second half sub.

The Viola took a shock lead about 10 minutes in, inevitably through Batistuta, but it seemed like a minor inconvenience. Midway through the first half Il Genio, Savicevic, had levelled the scores and set things back on their allotted path. Only Claudio Ranieri on the visitors' bench had other ideas.

With Rui Costa pulling the strings behind Batigol and Belgian-Brazilian hitman Lulu Oliveira there was always a chance of an upset if they could keep the scores level. Grafters like Stefan Schwarz, Sandro Cois and Giovanni Piacentini ensured that it did. Anything that got past them and the back four was dealt with by Francesco Toldo - the goalkeeeper who had started out his career with the Rossoneri and would finish it with their bitter rivals Inter.

In the 81st minute, Ranieri decided to play his joker and throw on lucky mascot Anselmo "Spadino" Robbiati in place of Rui Costa. Moments later the Viola won a free kick outside the penalty box just about in line with the goal post to Rossi's right hand side. There was never any question over who would take it.

The Viola's warrior unleashed a terrific blast which the Milan goalkeeper leaped after forlornly to try to keep out of his net. There was no stopping the ball, however, as it was drawn inexorably into the goal to give the Florentines their only victory in a Supercoppa final. A small crowd of about 30,000 made the San Siro seem a miserable place but there was bedlam among the travelling Florentines. "It's time up!" Rui Costa yelled to the referee from the sidelines in the closing stages and, eventually, he was proved right.

"We played like we know how at the home of the best team in the world," said Batigol after the game. "That is what fills us with pride."

"We really wanted to get a result," he added. "It was too important a chance for us to miss. You don't get many days like this. As for me, I got lucky, let's hope it continues."

"Fiorentina are now a real force," beamed Fiorentina President Vittorio Cecchi Gori. "We got the better of a more experienced Milan side. The Scudetto? Every game has a story of its own – the championship is a different matter."

"Now we have got to be smart and use this good run in our favour," said Ranieri. "If we can keep our feet on the ground, we can do well in the league as well."

"It was a good game," said Inter boss Roy Hodgson who had turned out to see his city rivals defeated. "They are two sides with different styles. Milan attacked more and wanted to impose themselves on the game while Fiorentina were more cautious and counter-attacked as well. The best players on the pitch were Boban, Savicevic and, of course, Batistuta."

The result turned out to be a warning signal for Milan who suffered a grim Serie A season and ended their title defence in the bottom half of the table. For the Viola it was the catalyst for a spending splurge by president Vittorio Cecchi Gori which saw them emerge as Champions League participants and serious Scudetto contenders. It would all end about five years down the line, of course, in financial disaster.

The game ushered in a spell when Fiorentina almost came to "own" the San Siro when visiting the Rossoneri. Between 1998 and 2001 they were undefeated in away ties to Milan, recording three victories and a draw - including a memorable 3-1 win courtesy of a Batigol hat-trick in that 1998/99 season where he nearly dragged them to the title. It was a happy hunting ground.

It would be only fair to point out that Milan have gained ample revenge. Some of their most resounding victories have come against Fiorentina. In the Viola's last season in Serie A before financial collapse they cuffed them 5-2 and they welcomed them back in 2004 with a 6-0 drubbing. Recent years have been more kind to the Tuscans, however, with a few famous victories in the San Siro. But whenever the two team go head to head, some of us will still have Batigol's words of love ringing in our ears.

Milan: Rossi; Reiziger, Costacurta, Baresi, Maldini; Albertini (76 Eranio), Desailly, Boban; Savicevic (66 Davids), Weah, Simone.

Fiorentina: Toldo; Carnasciali, Falcone, Firicano, Amoruso; Piacentini, Schwarz, Cois (92 Pusceddu), Rui Costa (81 Robbiati); Batistuta, Oliveira (86 Bigica).

Goals: 11 & 83 Batistuta, 21 Savicevic.

Catania v Inter

Stadio Cibali, 4 June 1961

The great pieces of sporting commentary can survive for generations. Sometimes a snappy phrase or saying can even outlive the pundit who first let it play across their lips. Little could the late, great Sandro Ciotti have imagined that his interruption of Tutto Il Calcio Minuto per Minuto (All the Football, Minute by Minute) on 4 June 1961 would remain so significant to this day. "Clamoroso al Cibali!" he cried. And at that very moment a classic piece of Calcio shorthand was created.

It might have been more than 50 years ago but – guess what? – Juve and Inter were locked in a bitter and vitriolic fight for the Scudetto. It would have a poisoned epilogue in the most farcical Derby d'Italia ever. However, when the Nerazzurri travelled to face Catania they still had some kind of shot at the title. But the Stadio Cibali (now the Angelo Massimino) proved to be an unexpected graveyard for their Scudetto dreams.

In truth, Inter's build up to the game had been far from ideal. They thought they were heading into the match on level terms with the Bianconeri but instead found themselves two points adrift. The meeting between the Nerazzurri and La Vecchia Signora earlier in the season had been suspended due to a huge crowd close to the pitch and the victory awarded to Helenio Herrera's side. However, that verdict was overturned on the eve of the Catania clash and the match ordered to be replayed. It still left Inter with a shot at the title, but many of the players claimed their minds were not on the job.

"We only heard the verdict that sent us slipping back to two points behind Juve when we were already in Catania," claimed Aristide Guarneri. "We went out onto the pitch with our morale at an all-time low. We felt we had been made fools of."

That, however, should not belittle what the home side achieved that day. They had been humbled earlier in the season by Herrera's men at the San Siro. They lost five goals without reply - an incredible four of them being own goals. It was reported that the Inter coach dubbed his opponents a bunch of postmen.

"After the way we played, maybe he was right," admitted Catania midfielder Memo Prenna. "Four own goals is a bit much. But we looked each other in the eyes and promised to gain revenge."

"Total surrender from Catania in the San Siro," was how one newsreel of the time described it. "Five-nil is a result which doesn't leave room for debate. For the winter champions, the Scudetto is not too far away."

It would prove, however, to be out of reach. Catania got their chance to put a spanner in the works on the final day of the season and they took it in style, despite claims that they were offered a financial incentive to lose a match they had no need to win. A memorable season saw the Sicilians already safely ensconced in midtable. But their hurt pride saw them play with fierce determination. It was the kind of end of season performance which remains unusual in Italy to this day. Results of convenience remain something of an embarrassment to Serie A. Catania showed they were not about to join the long list of teams who take their holidays early once their top division survival has been secured.

Winger Mario Castellazzi opened the scoring after 25 minutes. "I remember it well," he would recount many years later. "The Inter defence had cleared the ball but I stopped it on my chest and hit it first time into the top corner. They ruled out another one I scored and I hit the woodwork – it could have been 4-0."

But it was the second strike which would prompt Ciotti's exclamation. With 70 minutes on the clock Argentinian forward Salvador Calvanese grabbed a goal which pretty much put the match beyond doubt. With Juventus ahead at home to Bari (they would ultimately draw) the title was heading to Turin. Inter would send out their youth side - including a certain Sandro Mazzola - for the rearranged tie with Juve which now served no purpose at all.

"Catania put a stop to Inter's Scudetto dreams," wrote Vittorio Pozzo in his report on the game. "The Sicilian side had nothing to play for in the league but fought to avenge its defeat in the San Siro and to show good sportsmanship. The tempo of the men from Catania threw the plans of their opponents into disarray."

"The Nerazzurri were staring into the abyss," said a colourful match commentary of the era. "They even lost their second place to Milan, a season which could have been a triumph for Helenio Herrera's men ended up in a burning defeat."

There were reports that the home support goaded Inter with chants in favour of the Bianconeri. Certainly, they had gained more than a little revenge for their thrashing earlier in the campaign. Most viewers reckoned the loss could have been even heavier for the visitors.

"They didn't see much of the ball that day," recalled Amilcare Ferretti. "They told me that Luis Suarez, who Inter had bought for the following season, was in the ground that day. I had a great time, the Cibali was a hellish place for teams to visit – only Juventus won there that season."

Even though the ground no longer carries that name and the gravel-voiced commentator passed away a few years ago, the phrase "Clamoroso al Cibali!" has survived to this day. It has spawned a film and website and is now used to describe any shock result - particularly one achieved by a team which has no real reason to put up such a fight. They are all too rare in Italy, but Catania sure produced one more than half a century ago.

Catania: Gaspari; Michelotti, Giavara; Ferretti, Grani, Corti; Caceffo, Biagini, Calvanese, Prenna, Castellazzi.

Inter: Da Pozzo; Picchi, Facchetti; Bolchi, Guarneri, Balleri; Bicicli, Lindskog, Firmani, Corso, Morbello.

Goals: 25 Castellazzi, 70 Calvanese.

Juventus v Milan

Stadio Delle Alpi, 28 March 1998

They are two of the game's great executioners. Their preferred methods of delivering the coup de grace could hardly be more different, but they share the same efficient outcome. Back in 1998 it was Fabio Capello's Milan who were on the receiving end of a cold-blooded Calcio killing.

If you want a masterclass in the respective abilities of Alessandro Del Piero and Filippo Inzaghi you need look no further. His Juve shirt billowing in the breeze, a fresh-faced Pinturicchio delivered two delicious dead ball strikes. While Super Pippo - like crafty Jerry mouse sneaking off with the cheese - plundered a pair of goals before the offside trap could snap shut.

By week 27 of the 1997/98 season Marcello Lippi's men were locked in a three-way Scudetto tussle with Inter and Lazio. Nothing less than three points would do against a Rossoneri outfit struggling badly in mid-table. Few could have suspected, however, just how emphatic the outcome would be.

It was a hotchpotch Milan side which took to the Delle Alpi pitch that day. The remnants of the old guard stood side by side with young hopefuls and some never-would-amount-to-much professionals. The collective will of the Bianconeri would prove too much for them to stand.

Lippi's Juve were a tough nut for anyone to crack. Defenders like Paolo Montero looked about as warm and welcoming as Clint Eastwood in a cowboy film. And if you got past him there was Angelo Peruzzi - the Orangutan - ready to swing into action to stop any shots with his chunky frame.

Not that they were without their problems. Ciro Ferrara and Daniel Fonseca were ruled out with injury while future boss Antonio Conte was suspended. Zinedine Zidane was a doubt until the last minute and eventually ended up sitting on the sidelines.

With such a talent missing out, the Bianconeri opted to rack up the endeavour levels yet further with Alessio Tacchinardi in midfield alongside other footsoldiers like Angelo Di Livio and Edgar Davids. They produced a growling, grizzly display which had Milan cowering for cover.

Capello responded with a patchwork side that still had a spine of great names. Sebastiano Rossi in goal, Marcel Desailly and Paolo Maldini in defence, Roberto Donadoni and Zvoni Boban in midfield and George Weah up front were used to better things. Their supporting cast, sadly, was the stuff of nightmares.

Patrick Kluivert would never produce the goals for Milan he did elsewhere. Christian Zeige and Ibrahim Ba proved poor Stranieri. And Daniele Daino and Giovanni Cardone might be the weakest full-back pair the club has put out in the last 20 years.

The disastrous results did not take long to come. Within 12 minutes Rossi had felled an onrushing Davids in the penalty box to concede a spot kick. ADP kept his nerve to slot the ball home with great aplomb, sending the ball to the goalkeeper's left while he dived right.

That might have opened the floodgates there and then but referee Stefano Braschi returned the favour to the Rossoneri about 20 minutes later. He judged Gianluca Pessotto to have upended Weah and pointed to the spot once again. It was Zorro Boban's turn to keep his cool and his angled shot beat Peruzzi despite the shotstopper diving the right way. There was a lot of pent-up rage in the Croatian's goal celebrations.

The joy for the travelling Milanese support would prove to be short-lived, however, as Del Piero completed a double before half-time. He won a free-kick himself just outside the penalty area a little to the left of goal. And he made it seem like child's play to curl the ball into the far corner away from the despairing gloves of Rossi. It was his 19th of the season.

"You can't give him so many chances from free kicks," said former Milan goalie Giovanni Galli in the commentary box. "He might miss once, he might even miss twice but the third time he will punish you."

If things looked bad for Milan at that point, they only got worse five minutes later. Boban took a kick at Davids and was given his marching orders just before the half-time whistle blew. The boys in red and black were falling to pieces and they still had 45 minutes to suffer. Capello tried some running repairs at the interval, bringing on Giampiero Maini and Steinar Nilson for Kluivert and Daino but it did little to stop the Juve forwards flooding towards goal.

The situation put the match in the perfect position for an Inzaghi show. With the Rossoneri under more and more pressure, the goal grabber par excellence was in his element. He happily pounced on a couple of defensive distractions.

On the hour mark he was put clear by Didier Deschamps and expertly rounded Rossi to roll the ball into the net. Then, with only seven minutes to play, he perfectly controlled a beautiful through ball from Fabio Pecchia to thump home his second. It was game, set and match to Juve and a decisive step towards the Scudetto.

"Irresistible Juve!" proclaimed La Gazzetta dello Sport. With 33 goals between them, Del Piero and Inzaghi were proving too hot for most defences to handle. Their manager was, understandably, delighted.

"Our forwards are playing incredibly well," he admitted. "Del Piero and Inzaghi are confirming their characteristics. One, Inzaghi, is deadly at sticking it in the net, taking the slightest chance, always ready to pounce and always first to the ball.

"The other, Del Piero, has a complete array of qualities which you could sum up as follows - technique, class, cunning, smartness, speed of execution and a repertoire of extraordinary goalscoring trajectories.

"The truth is, their teammates are setting up Del Piero and Inzaghi perfectly. They have understood they have to play to each one's strengths."

It proved to be a winning formula as the Milan victory was the first of a run of five wins which would guarantee the title. The last of the sequence was the infamous clash with Inter when a penalty was not given to the Nerazzurri for a foul on Ronaldo inside the box. That would forever cloud the title in some people's eyes - but not those of a Bianconero persuasion. They were too busy savouring yet another Scudetto. And one in which their two goalscoring assassins had played a deadly part.

Juventus: Peruzzi; Torricelli, Iuliano, Montero (67 Birindelli), Pessotto (81 Dimas); Di Livio, Tacchinardi (74 Pecchia), Deschamps, Davids; Inzaghi, Del Piero.

Milan: Rossi; Daino (46 Nilsen), Desailly, Maldini, Cardone; Ba (61 Leonardo), Donadoni, Boban, Ziege; Kluivert (46 Maini), Weah.

Goals: 12 Del Piero (pen), 33 Boban (pen), 40 Del Piero, 60 & 83 Inzaghi.

Genoa v Inter

Stadio Luigi Ferraris, 12 May 1991

Few fans present in the Stadio Luigi Ferraris had seen such a result before. It had been more than three decades since their favourites had managed to win a home Serie A match against Inter. But, in May 1991, Genoa ended that long-running hoodoo in swashbuckling style.

It was a case of the upstart side against the established elite. Just a couple of seasons earlier, Giovanni Trapattoni's Inter side with its colony of German internationals (they already had Lothar Matthaus and Andy Brehme and would add Jurgen Klinsmann later) had won the Scudetto with a record-breaking points total. At the same time, the boys from the Marassi had been scrapping their way out of Serie B.

By 1991, however, there was a case for saying Serie A was about as wide open as it has ever been. Maradona's Napoli were reigning champions, Arrigo Sacchi's Milan had been conquering Europe, Sampdoria were a major force with Vialli and Mancini. Sides like Parma and Torino, too, had serious European ambitions. It was a cut-throat time for Calcio.

Inter had given it their best shot to have a crack at the title, standing toe-to-toe with Samp for much of the season. But the round of matches before their trip to Genoa had seen them lose 2-0 to Doria, effectively ending their Scudetto aspirations. They also had the distraction of an upcoming return leg of their UEFA Cup final with Roma. With Osvaldo Bagnoli's men determined to grab a European place of their own, there was plenty of incentive for victory. Few could have predicted just how emphatic it would turn out to be.

Trapattoni was unable or unwilling to risk a full strength team for the match. Stalwart defender Beppe Bergomi, aerial target man Aldo Serena and German full-back Andy Brehme were all missing for the match. And things would only get worse as the game progressed.

A knock to Beppe Baresi forced him to leave the fray too and be replaced by Paolo Stringara. Still the visitors' defence held strong for most of the first half, with most of the danger to Walter Zenga's goal coming from free-kicks by lethal Brazilian Branco. Eventually, however, they were undone by two of Genoa's midfield motor-men.

Gennaro Ruotolo picked up the ball and ran on to a return pass from Mario Bortolazzi to slice open the Inter back line. He produced a sweet, low finish to break the deadlock in the 38th minute. It was a vital turn of events which the boys in blue and black never looked like turning round.

The home side looked the more hungry and it was to be little-and-large strike duo of Czech Tomas Skuhravy and Uruguayan Pato Aguilera who completed the rout. In the 76th minute it was a drifting cross from the South American which his European counterpart looped over Zenga with a perfect header. Then, late in the game, it was Skuhravy who went flying in the penalty box with Aguilera duly converting the spot kick.

Post-match, Trapattoni looked disappointed but not too downhearted. He knew his club had other priorities for the season and were playing a side which had more reason to push for the points.

"We were up against an opponent who gave us nothing," he said. "We had some key players missing, even if that's no excuse. But Bergomi, Serena and Brehme are not the kind of players you can replace easily and some of the players coming in were not in top condition. By the end, a few of our players looked tired too."

"Genoa were worth the win, we can have no complaints," admitted the gentlemanly coach. "The game was fairly balanced up until Ruotolo got his goal but after than Genoa left us trailing and we drowned in our own tiredness."

But the tactical maestro did have a few words to say for the critics who thought he left his team fatally imbalanced by replacing the more defensively-minded Andrea Mandorlini with striker Maurizio Iorio with about 15 minutes left to play and just a goal between the sides.

"It would be easy to say I made a mistake sending on a third striker but by that stage it really didn't matter if we conceded one or three goals, the important thing was to try to get back into the game," he said. "We tried but our physical decline was pretty clear. As soon as we pushed forward, Genoa punished us in style."

"The level of motivation was different," claimed the Grifone's towering skipper Gianluca Signorini. "For us, playing Inter is always an extra boost and our concentration was total. We played a perfect game today." It is sad to think that a little more than a decade after celebrating such a great season, their influential captain would succumb to Lou Gehrig's disease aged just 42.

Genoa coach Bagnoli reckoned he had got his tactics about right. "We knew Inter were strong - although without Serena they lost something at free-kicks," he said. "But with Fausto Pizzi in the team we thought they would try to outmanoeuvre us.

"But the moment we got the ball we had to break quickly," he added. "We could not allow them to break with the kind of players they have like Nicola Berti, Lothar Matthaus and the likes. We were very concentrated, we were in good form and we got the first goal which helped us out too.

"I don't usually single out players but let me say that I thought Skuhravy made the difference today," continued Bagnoli. "And in the closing stages, with Ferri struggling, things got even easier for him."

The result would help to clinch historic UEFA Cup qualification for Genoa at the end of the season while Inter would go into the same competition as holders after seeing off Roma. The Nerazzurri's defence of that crown would not go particularly well with early elimination to Boavista. The Rossoblu, however, went all the way to the semi-final before missing out to Ajax who would also conquer Torino in the final.

As for the jinx-breaking victory over Inter, it did not really herald a golden age at home to the Milanese giants for the Grifone. They still, generally, lose more games with the Nerazzurri at the Marassi than they win, but the balance of power has certainly shifted a little. There will surely never be another era when they have to wait more than a quarter century to savour such a success.

Genoa: Braglia; Torrente, Signorini, Caricola, Branco; Onorati, Bortolazzi (89 Fiorin), Ruotolo, Eranio; Aguilera, Skuhravy.

Inter: Zenga; Paganin, Battistini, Baresi (17 Stringara), Ferri; Pizzi, Bianchi, Mandorlini (74 Iorio), Berti; Matthaus, Klinsmann.

Goals: 36 Ruotolo, 76 Skuhravy, 89 Aguilera (pen).

Lazio v Fiorentina

Stadio Olimpico, 10 May 1998

They were the kind of players who could dance around defenders. If the battering ram of Gabriel Batistuta let Fiorentina down they turned to their mesmerising feet. One May day in Rome, Luis "Lulu" Oliveira, Manuel Rui Costa and Edmundo ran riot.

In truth, that Lazio against Fiorentina clash in 1998 was all about motivation. The Viola needed the win to clinch a place in the following season's UEFA Cup, the Biancocelesti had already switched off for the season. It showed in their display.

Sven Eriksson's men had been heavily involved on a number of fronts. They won the Coppa Italia in late April, defeating Milan in the two-legged final. But they were humbled by the other side of the city, Inter, in the UEFA Cup final in Paris. To ask them to raise their game for the visit of Alberto Malesani's side was almost impossible. And they singularly failed to do so.

Lazio thought they might have had a penalty in the opening exchanges but, after that, the Tuscan side took control. A typically crunching midfield tackle from Sandro Cois sent the Belgian-Brazilian striker Oliveira into the clear. He opened his stance perfectly to spin a shot past Luca Marchegiani from wide on the left of the goal. The game was almost over as a contest already.

Oliveira turned provider in the 24th minute when he once again skipped away on the left. He swung in an inviting cross which Edmundo had no bother slamming home. The player dubbed "O Animal" spun away in celebration as if dancing at the carnival in Rio.

Pavel Nedved tried to rouse the home side with a cracking free kick which had Francesco Toldo beaten but also drifted past the post. It would be as close as Lazio would get to reopening the game. Batigol soon slammed the shutters in their face.

Giuseppe Favalli lost a high, bouncing ball in the sunlight and the Argentinian punished him severely. He did what he always did and powered a low, unstoppable shot goalwards. Any hope of a comeback had long since disappeared for the Roman side.

Indeed, it was only a self-inflicted wound which gave them any consolation. A looping cross from Nedved was met in powerful fashion by Michele Serena. His header gave his own goalkeeper no chance and it made the scoreline a more respectable 3-1.

The second half saw Gigi Casiraghi given his marching orders for complaining to the ref and the game began to drift away. But there was still time for a masterclass in style - and who else could provide it but the Viola's Portuguese ace? Rui Costa did not score as many goals as he should have but, when he did, they were usually pretty memorable. This time he taunted and teased Alessandro Grandoni before hitting home a sweet long-range effort. It was the icing on the cake for the Florentine outfit.

"I am sorry, but I hope the fans remember all the good things we have done up until a few months ago," said Lazio boss Eriksson. "The defeat against Juventus in the league was fatal for us – when the chance of a place in the Champions League went, we lost our concentration. Then the injuries to our defenders, midfielders and the prolonged absence of Boksic did the rest."

"I'll be honest, I am ashamed," added defender Paolo Negro. "We did not go out there to deliberately lose four goals. We started off quite well but after that I don't know exactly what happened."

Team-mate Roberto Mancini was a bit more understanding about the situation. "Nobody should be ashamed," he insisted. "After 54 games you have to accept anything, even a bit of tiredness. Lazio have never played two finals before and you shouldn't forget we had a couple of chances to go top of the league."

Rival fans, of course, took great glee in the Biancocelesti's failure to add to their Coppa Italia crown with a league title and UEFA Cup which had also been within reach at one stage of the season. One fan of their city rivals took to the air to fly a banner over the ground with the legend. *"Cucu', scudetto e coppa non ce so' piu'. Forza Roma!"* – "Cuckoo, the Scudetto and the Cup are gone. Forza Roma!". It was a harsh verdict on such a near-miss season for the capital club.

The game was a disappointing penultimate league fixture in an otherwise impressive season for the Laziali. They would use the campaign as a springboard to win the final edition of the Cup Winners' Cup the following year and follow it up with a European Super Cup triumph and then the Scudetto in 2000.

As for Fiorentina, their President Vittorio Cecchi Gori was unimpressed with what he had seen despite the convincing win and qualification for Europe. He had bigger things in mind and his post-match statement hinted that change was in the air on the Viola bench. "Europe is the very least we should have achieved," he told reporters and it was pretty clear that Malesani's days were numbered. Sure enough, Giovanni Trapattoni would take over at the Tuscan club the following season.

They did not make much of an impact in the UEFA Cup after clinching qualification in Rome. They saw off Hadjuk Split in the first round but a firework which hit a match official in their second round clash with Grasshoppers effectively ended their involvement. The game was being played in Salerno due to a previous ban imposed on the Stadio Franchi in Florence and it later emerged it had been locals rather than Viola fans who had thrown the offending item. Nonetheless, the game was awarded 3-0 to the Swiss side, overturning Fiorentina's 2-0 lead from the away leg. It was a sorry conclusion to a story which had started with such a rhythmical and impressive display in the Stadio Olimpico.

Lazio: Marchegiani; Grandoni, Nesta, Negro, Favalli; Fuser, Venturin (52 Gottardi), Jugovic (49 Almeyda), Nedved (83 Marcolin); Casiraghi, Mancini.

Fiorentina: Toldo; Tarozzi, Firicano, Padalino; Serena, Cois, Rui Costa (87 Carta), Amoroso; Edmundo (84 Morfeo), Batistuta, Oliveira (84 Robbiati).

Goals: 12 Oliveira, 24 Edmundo, 41 Batistuta, 42 Serena (og), 85 Rui Costa.

Parma v Milan

Stadio Ennio Tardini, 20 January 1991

Every era of Italian football had a scalp most teams would like to claim. In the 1960s it was usually Helenio Herrera's Inter side and a decade later Giovanni Trapattoni's Juve had definitely seized that crown. But, by the end of the 1980s, there was little doubt Arrigo Sacchi's Milan were a prized victory in any club's season. To beat them in your Serie A debut campaign? Unthinkable, surely.

But Nevio Scala's Parma were the little team who dreamed big. He had taken the groundwork done by, among others, Sacchi himself and turned the Tardini terrors into Serie B promotion material. By the time they got into the top flight they were more than ready to start bringing more illustrious names down a peg or two.

Still, their chances of beating the freshly crowned World Club Champions in January 1991 seemed more slender than the elegant Marco Osio. Sure, the Gialloblu were a team with a tactical blueprint and a gameplan which was very well tried and tested but they were going up against one of the best outfits of all time. Franco Baresi, Billy Costacurta, Frank Rijkaard, Ruud Gullit and Marco Van Basten would all step out onto the pitch in Parma to defend the red and black colours.

It would start badly and end worse, however, for the Rossoneri and, in particular, a more-emotionally-involved-than-most Carlo Ancelotti. It was his first chance to lock horns in Serie A with the side where he emerged as a potential star at both club and international level. An uncharacteristic blunder let an in-form hitman break the deadlock with just a few minutes on the clock.

"The ball went between my legs and Alessandro Melli was behind me and hit it into the top corner," said the future manager of both teams. "These things happen in football but, when they do, it is sad."

Try as they might, Milan could not get their trademark pressing play going and Sacchi cut a forlorn figure as he sat in the stands serving a suspension. Scala's side were able to sit in and break at pace and with great intent. It was no surprise when Melli doubled the home side's lead before half time - taking him to double figures at the halfway point of the season.

"Ten goals are a lot and nine of them have come from open play," said the striker. "I am very pleased with my first half of this campaign but the best thing was seeing this Parma team beat the champions of the world. Everybody talks about Melli, Brolin and Osio but nobody speaks about our defence. Nowadays to score against Parma is harder than scoring against Milan."

The Rossoneri tried their best to break down that backline in the second half but they struggled to produce much in the way of attacking threat. Ancelotti was replaced with Roberto Donadoni who had been an injury doubt before kick-off but it made little difference. Even when they did cut the Parma defence open they struggled to get a clean strike on goal. Indeed, the game fizzled out with a feeble tumble by Donadoni in an attempt to win a penalty in the closing minutes a symbol of Milan's performance. It earned him a yellow card for his troubles and summed up a match in which it was possible for one report to carry the headline "Super Melli outshines Van Basten."

"We didn't play badly," insisted Costacurta after the game. "But when you don't manage a single shot on goal it is no use complaining."

"We had a bit of luck to score early and that maybe upset Milan," admitted Scala. "But Parma played an almost perfect game."

"Parma force their way among the big boys!" trumpeted La Stampa and it was impossible to argue with that assessment. They had shown they could mix it with one of the country's top sides and come out on top. It confirmed that they would be a team which needed to be taken seriously in times to come.

"The Parma side hitting the headlines today has been built this way – with just a few additions to the team that won promotion to Serie A for the first time," insisted Scala. "There is no secret – just determination, possession, courage and tactical awareness. By the halfway point in the season we have faced everyone and we have felt we are the equal of all our opponents – even Juventus who won here on the opening day. In fact, that absolutely undeserved defeat only served to make us even more determined." The newspapers reckoned his team – assembled at a fraction of the cost of many of its rivals – had quadrupled in value. And they would only go from strength to strength.

"We did not play like we can," admitted Baresi after the match. "While Parma did really well and made good use of the ball every time they had it. But if you don't try to shoot it is pretty hard to win a game. However, we can't be too downhearted, we've got a game in hand to try to sort things out."

The result at the Ennio Tardini would be a flavour of things to come for the Rossoneri in a frustrating conclusion to their season. Having been fighting at the table top before Christmas, their challenge slowly faded as Sampdoria clinched a historic Scudetto. A bid to win the European Cup for the third year in a row ended in embarrassment when the lights went out in Marseilles. Sacchi would soon be packing his bags for the Italy job.

As for Parma, they finished the season in sixth place - ahead of the likes of Juventus, Napoli and Roma. It was a calling card which would set the standard for the rest of the decade. A swashbuckling side went on to gather a string of trophies both at home and in Europe.

That all came crashing down, of course, when a multi-billion euro hole emerged in the books of main backer Parmalat in December 2003. The team has had to live on more modest means in recent times and has rarely threatened to scale the heights of its glory days. They recently marked the 100th anniversary of their formation as the Verdi Football Club in 1913 - but many of their most precious memories come from the side that beat Milan in Serie A at the first time of asking.

Parma: Taffarel; Donati, Grun, Minotti, Apolloni, Gambaro; Osio (74 Monza), Zoratto, Cuoghi; Melli (87 Mannari), Brolin.

Milan: Pazzagli; Tassotti, Costacurta, Baresi, Carobbi; Stroppa, Rijkaard, Ancelotti (46 Donadoni), Carbone; Gullit, Van Basten (68 Massaro).

Goals: 6 & 34 Melli.

Bologna v Juventus

Stadio Renato Dall'Ara, 6 November 1988

The late 1980s was a time of coaching revolution in Italy. Few have forgotten the transformation enacted by Arrigo Sacchi at Milan or Zdenek Zeman's cavalier Foggia side. Not so many remember Gigi Maifredi's little masterpiece at Bologna.

His move to the Rossoblu job in the summer of 1987 was little more than a footnote on the sports pages. He had successfully taken Ospitaletto to promotion to Serie C1 which was enough to convince the famous Emilia-Romagna club to snap him up. It prompted a protest from the Italian Manager's Association as he did not yet have the necessary qualifications to take over at a Serie B side. Nonetheless, the move went ahead.

Maifredi was quickly seen as a second Sacchi. His style was dubbed "champagne football" as a tribute to its exciting approach and his own background in the wine business. Like Arrigo, he was another coach from outside the traditional football world who was shaking up the game.

Things certainly fizzed in his first season at the Dall'Ara. The Bolognese sparkled in the second division and won it at a canter scoring plenty of goals along the way. The end of the season was accompanied by the pop of corks and a clink of glasses as they won promotion as champions.

That performance grabbed the attention of the club where Maifredi definitely saw himself ending up - Juventus. They were meditating a move like Milan's approach for Sacchi which had proved such a success. Could the Bologna boss be the man to add some extra style to the Bianconeri's play?

In the end, the Turin giants hesitated. In the summer of 1988 they went for the more obvious option of club legend Dino Zoff. They would come calling again for Maifredi at a later date but, in the meantime, he carried on his work at the Stadio Dall'Ara.

Arrival in Serie A was not easy. An opening day win over Pisa was a false dawn as top division sides proved more than capable of coping with Gigi's brand of exciting football. Three consecutive defeats were not the ideal build-up for the visit of Juventus in week five of the season.

Maifredi chose to cover-up and play a more defensive line-up than usual. He stuck to his zonal guns but tried to shore up the back line to better fend off the attacking talents of the likes Alessandro Altobelli, Michael Laudrup, Rui Barros and Sasha Zavarov. It singularly failed to work out.

Zoff's men were ahead within 15 minutes. An Altobelli assist saw little Portuguese Rui Barros show his usual quick wits to chip goalkeeper Nello Cusin - brought in from Ospitaletto along with Maifredi. It was the opener of a genuine goal glut with both defences all over the place.

Going behind saw Maifredi decide that his more cautious approach had not been rewarded. He took off another Ospitaletto import (and future Juve man) Marco De Marchi and threw on forward Giuseppe Lorenzo. But before half time the expert ex-Inter man Altobelli turned finisher and extended Juve's lead when he met a Zavarov cross to nod home.

"This Bologna side, thanks to Maifredi, seems happy to lose as long as its play gets plaudits and applause," wrote one slightly snide match report. It certainly looked like they were out of their depth when they went 3-0 down when Barros struck again (although some credit it as an own goal to Belgian import Stephane Demol). The home fans in the Dall'Ara were openly applauding, right enough, but it was Juve's play - not that of their own players.

Eventually, however, the Rossoblu started to show that their commitment to attacking football did involve a goalscoring threat as well as a leaky defence. Fabio Poli finally narrowed the gap, only for Laudrup to strike again to restore Juve's three-goal advantage. In the old days, the Bianconeri would have shut up shop at that stage but they had defensive frailties of their own.

It was an on-loan Juventino, Angelo Alessio, who gave the game a final twist. He came on and hit a quick-fire double which had the visitors' legs trembling. He only scored four goals all season for the Rossoblu, but half of them came against the club which owned him. There was visible relief in the Bianconeri ranks when the final whistle blew to clinch their win.

"We have to take a lot of the blame on all four goals," said Maifredi afterwards. "You need to pay more attention in Serie A."

"When a team tries to win, it opens up a bit," added Juve netminder Stefano Tacconi, in explanation of the goal glut. "But the important thing is scoring one goal more than your rivals."

Despite the defeat, Bologna were probably more happy with their season by its conclusion than Juve were. Zoff's men finished fourth as their defensive problems cost them dear while the Emilia-Romagna side dodged relegation by a couple of points. Maifredi's work could continue in the top division for another year.

The following season he managed an even more impressive eighth place finish which took Bologna into the UEFA Cup. With Juve finishing fourth once more, they decided the time was right to move for their man. Maifredi moved north in 1990 for his dream appointment with the Turin giants. It turned into a bit of a disaster.

In that single season with the Bianconeri he achieved something which had been impossible for a generation and managed to fail to qualify for Europe. It was enough to convince the club's hierarchy to put the cork back on champagne football. Giovanni Trapattoni was called upon to make his return to the helm.

As for Maifredi, his stock never quite recovered. He went back to Bologna but the magic had gone and he ended up travelling around Italy, Europe and even north Africa to try to restore his reputation. It never really worked and he now has a role on the technical staff with Brescia. But there is still a little twinkle in his eye when asked about his days with Bologna.

Bologna: Cusin; Monza, Villa, Luppi, De Marchi (22 Lorenzo); Stringara (46 Alessio), Pecci, Bonini, Demol; Poli, Marronaro.

Juventus: Tacconi; Favero, Brio, Tricella, Galia; Barros (82 Magrin), Zavarov, Marocchi, De Agostini; Laudrup, Altobelli.

Goals: 16 Barros, 42 Altobelli, 52 Demol (og), 65 Poli, 75 Laudrup, 82 & 88 Alessio.

Inter v Milan
Stadio San Siro, 6 November 1949

It was a time when most tales were told in black and white. The fledgling Italian democracy was struggling to find its feet under Alcide De Gasperi. At cinemas, the hot ticket was for Il Mulino del Po based on Riccardo Bacchelli's epic family saga of the same name. And, in the remote countryside, the bodies left by the Second World War were still being found.

In the football world, Serie A was still coming to terms with the loss of the Grande Torino side at the Superga disaster. It left a power vacuum which a number of sides hoped to fill. That honour went, as it so often has, to Juventus, Inter and Milan.

In the 1949/50 campaign, the 10th week of matches threw up a mouthwatering prospect. A great Bianconero outfit - the one with Giampiero Boniperti, John Hansen, Karl Praest and the likes - was setting a breakneck speed at the top of the table followed by surprise outfit Padova. The Milanese giants were locked together in third place, four points adrift of top spot. The winner of the derby at the San Siro would be making a statement of its intent to target the Scudetto.

Inter were the home side for this league clash and boasted a breathtaking attack. France-born Hungarian Istvan Nyers was a 30-goals-a-season kind of guy. "He had a turn of pace which was deadly," recalled former team-mate Sergio Brighenti. "It made him unstoppable. He could shoot with either foot, knew where the goal was and had the courage of a lion." Among his forward colleagues were ex-Roma hero Amedeo Amadei and the Tuscan they nicknamed *Veleno* (Poison) for his venomous finishes and prickly personality, Benito Lorenzi. Their defensive powers, however, were weakened by the loss of a certain Enzo Bearzot to injury a week earlier against Novara.

The Rossoneri responded with a side with even greater goal potential. It boasted three men whose names would eventually be moulded into one famous abbreviation. Gunnar Gren, Gunnar Nordahl and Nils Liedholm. Gre-No-Li for short.

The Italian league had just confirmed a limit of three foreign players in its sides. The Swedish trio formed Milan's contingent while Dutchman Faas Wilkes joined Nyers in the Inter starting XI that day. There was no spot for Argentinian Oscar Basso, their third Straniero.

These were days before Catenaccio had raised its head and both sides lined up along the 2-3-2-3 lines of the Metodo system. In a time when foreign coaches were in vogue, Hungarian Lajos Czeizler guided the Rossoneri but the much more Italian man from Massa Giulio Cappelli was in charge at Inter. They dished up what might well have been a tactical expert's nightmare but proved to be a football fan's delight.

It was obvious from pretty early on that this would be no ordinary Derby della Madonnina, there would be no cagey exchanges or worrying about keeping things tight at the back. The first goal came in the opening minute and it was Milan who seized the advantage through former Inter man Enrico Candiani. He doubled his personal tally, and the Rossoneri's lead, before seven minutes had passed.

In the 10th minute, Inter clawed one back through Nyers but it looked like the "visitors" were in outright control when Nordahl and Liedholm extended their lead to 4-1. There were less than 20 minutes on the clock and one of the biggest derby games in Europe looked effectively over as a contest. But these were days of more epic scorelines and the Nerazzurri had an astounding comeback in mind.

It was constructed either side of half-time. In a vital one-two in the space of a minute, Amadei and a Nyers penalty narrowed the gap before the interval. Then, incredibly, Amadei levelled the match five minutes into the second period. It was 4-4 and any outcome looked possible at the final whistle.

The ever-sharp Lorenzi put Inter into the lead for the first time a little shy of the hour mark but Milan showed resilience of their own to hit back immediately through Carlo Annovazzi. It would take just five more minutes for the match to make its final fateful twist. Amadei was the gamewinner as he grabbed his hat-trick to complete an improbable scoreline. Lorenzi danced a provocative dribble as the final whistle blew before kicking the ball into the delighted and still slightly stunned Inter faithful. It remains, not surprisingly, the highest scoreline in a Serie A Milanese derby.

"Was this a good game or a bad game?" asked one match report. "We tried to reach a judgement on that but it was not straightforward. The match had everything - spectacular attacking and defences which collapsed like barriers built from papier-mâché, a team which conceded four goals in a row after building up a three-goal lead and two sides which mixed great play with amateur errors."

"There was a day, many years ago, when Torino and Inter drew 6-6 but there was a downpour that day and the terrible pitch conditions caused all the problems," wrote double World Cup-winning coach Vittorio Pozzo in his analysis. "Six goals are nice for the Inter attack and five strikes are sweet for the Milan forward line but they are disastrous for the two defences. They are a bit of an indicator of the state of these Milanese sides - they have scored 29 and 25 goals respectively but conceded 16 and 17. The defenders of the city of Milan ruined their reputation on Sunday."

There was not much time to rest for some of the protagonists. Amadei, Lorenzi and Inter team-mates Osvaldo Fattori and Attilio Giovannini were called up to the Italy training squad for a match with England later in the month along with Annovazzi of Milan. Then there was the little matter of Juventus versus Inter the following weekend.

The Bianconeri would win another humdinger of a clash 3-2 and set sail towards the title. Milan would emerge as their closest rivals but still finished five points adrift in second spot with Inter a further eight points behind in third. The Rossoneri racked up 118 goals that campaign with Nordahl scoring 35 alone. Inter ended up just shy of the century with 99 strikes - 30 of them from Nyers.

Neither side would have to wait long for a title. Milan were crowned champions the following season and Inter secured the Scudetto by 1953. It set a trend for domination which - along with Juve of course - has continued for most of the modern history of the Italian game. And perhaps a little bit of that supremacy had its roots in the lessons learned from the most madcap derby in the city's history.

Inter: Franzosi; Guait, Miglioli; Campatelli, Giovannini, Achilli; Amadei, Wilkes, Lorenzi, Fiorini, Nyers.

Milan: Milanese; De Gregori, Foglia; Annovazzi, Tognon, Bonomi; Burini, Gren, Nordahl, Liedholm, Candiani.

Goals: 1 & 7 Candiani, 10 & 40 (pen) Nyers, 14 Nordahl, 19 Liedholm, 39, 50 & 64 Amadei, 58 Lorenzi, 59 Annovazzi.

Verona v Chievo

Stadio Marcantonio Bentegodi, 18 November 2001

Alberto Malesani is not a man to keep his feelings to himself. When it comes to celebrating a victory in style, he has plenty of Serie A history. But few games gave him more pleasure than the first ever Verona derby in Italy's highest division.

The backstory, as almost everyone knows by now, centred on a traditional British summertime seaside mode of transport - the donkey. Hellas fans reckoned those creatures would have to take to the air before city rivals Chievo reached the top flight. When they eventually did so, they adopted the Flying Donkey as their nickname to mock their cousins.

So to say there was eager anticipation for the clash in Verona in November 2001 would be something of an understatement. With Hellas the home side, the Bentegodi was resplendent in blue and gold for the game. To add a little extra flavour, newly-promoted Chievo had made such an impact in Serie A that they actually had the audacity to be sitting top of the table. Malesani's men were no slouches either, sitting in a very respectable midtable position.

It is easy to forget just how impressive Gigi Delneri's 4-4-2 formation was. With its flying wide men, it shook up the established order from day one in the division. They quickly became the team most of the big guns wanted to avoid, such was their lack of respect for reputations. Newly promoted sides in Italy were simply not supposed to behave in such an enterprising manner.

Malesani's Verona were a nice outfit too, especially the attacking options for his 3-4-3 line-up. Mauro Camoranesi and Adrian Mutu were a sumptuous duo to have in operation on either side of a central striker. A few eyebrows might be raised in hindsight, however, by the fact that he opted for Lichtenstein's finest Mario Frick to start the city derby ahead of a future goalscoring legend like Alberto Gilardino.

The game was played out under driving rain and with the kind of passion and commitment you would expect of such a historic match. It was Delneri's side who called the shots in the opening period with a goal disallowed before the man known then as Eriberto - but Luciano nowadays - broke the deadlock shortly after the half-hour mark. When ex-Verona man Eugenio Corini converted a penalty a few minutes later, it looked like the donkeys would be taking to the skies once more.

But Verona got a penalty lifeline before the break which Massimo Oddo duly converted. It was just enough encouragement to get the home team flying out of the traps in the second half. Mutu - just back from disappointing defeat in a World Cup qualifier play-off with his country - was in particularly fine form.

It would be Chievo striker Massimo Marazzina who played an unwanted key role when he got himself sent off for a pointless tackle from behind on the hour mark. Then, as if the self-harm had not gone far enough, Salvatore Lanna thumped one past his own keeper, Cristiano Lupatelli. To complete an improbable comeback, Camoranesi beat a poor offside trap to knock home the winner. The Hellas fans, and Malesani, could not contain their joy.

"This was a hymn to football," opined La Repubblica in its match report. "It was the first derby in Serie A between Verona and Chievo but we can only hope there will be plenty more if they are going to be so packed with good football and excitement – including the odd error. The game ended with Malesani being carried in triumph to the Curva Nord and leaving the pitch in his vest."

Those celebrations under the Curva are the stuff of Bentegodi legend. He jumped with joy, he waved in delight and then threw off his training coat in an impromptu striptease. Not everyone thought his actions were appropriate.

"I don't care what people think," he retorted. "I wanted to behave like that and I did. I am happy for this victory. I don't give a s**t if I have only won the Verona derby and not the Scudetto. Maybe people will say that's why I can't manage a big team.

"But I only do this once every three years while others talk nonsense every weekend and nobody criticises them. Sport is there to be enjoyed - it is joy and happiness. There were people in the crowd who live near my home, who I could go and have a glass of wine with in an osteria. I wanted to share my great satisfaction."

"Even if I had won I wouldn't have gone to my fans to celebrate," said a glum Delneri. "What matters is that my team fought hard and I don't think they come out of this game devalued. I don't talk about referee decisions but there is no doubt sometimes in football it is episodes which decide a game. There are a few things I found hard to swallow, but I'll keep them to myself."

He was correct in his assessment that his team still had plenty to give in its debut Serie A campaign. They slipped off top spot but still managed an impressive fifth place finish which took them into the UEFA Cup. They also got revenge in the return fixture later in the season.

Indeed, it was the Flying Donkeys who had the last laugh overall. Hellas slumped from a strong start and tumbled down the table to end up in the last relegation spot alongside Venezia, Fiorentina and Lecce. Malesani might have regretted the exuberance of his celebrations at winning Serie A's first Veronese derby. Then again, looking back at what he said at the time, you have to reckon he wouldn't change a single thing about the day.

Verona: Ferron; Cannavaro, Zanchi, Gonnella (65 Salvetti); Oddo, Italiano, Colucci, Seric; Camoranesi (87 Dossena), Frick (77 Gilardino), Mutu.

Chievo: Lupatelli; Foglio, Legrottaglie, D'Anna, Lanna; Eriberto (65 Mayele), Perrotta, Corini, Manfredini (82 Beghetto); Corradi (73 Cossato), Marazzina.

Goals: 33 Eriberto, 37 Corini (pen), 40 Oddo (pen), 70 Lanna (og), 72 Camoranesi.

Milan v Udinese

Stadio Giuseppe Meazza, 8 January 1984

It was a midtable encounter with a classy cast. The protagonists were a mix of old glories and stars of the future. And they produced a memorable encounter on the famous San Siro turf in January 1984.

Milan had just returned from their second spell in Serie B in a couple of seasons and were definitely a team still under construction. The Silvio Berlusconi era had not yet begun and the dubious star Straniero of the team was former Watford hitman Luther Blissett. The Englishman would amass just five goals all season.

The visitors, Udinese, had a foreigner with a little more glamour attached. Arthur Antunes Coimbra, better known as Zico, had incredibly been convinced to trade Flamengo for the Friuli in the summer of 1983. He quickly developed an excellent understanding with his World Cup rival of the year before, Franco Causio.

Under Ilario Castagner the Rossoneri had suffered a dreadfully inconsistent start to their season. Their first four home games ended in victory but their first four away matches led to defeat. They started to show a bit of more solid form before Christmas but, even so, they were five points adrift of league-leading Juventus by the time Udinese came to town.

Their visitors came into the game undefeated since the end of November and had just dished out a memorable 4-1 drubbing to Napoli. They sat on the same points as the Milanese giants. A good result could be a turning point for either side.

Things got off to the best possible start for the home team when they benefitted from one of those soft penalties which have never gone out of fashion in Italy. Sergio Battistini took a tumble in the box and Franco Baresi duly stepped up to convert the spot-kick. The Udinese defence looked shaky with the likes of Attilio Tesser and Franco Pancheri missing.

The Rossoneri looked like they had things under control with Mauro Tassotti tracking Zico, Filippo Galli taking care of Pietro Virdis and Alberigo

Evani asked to deal with the dribbling skills of Causio. It worked for more than half an hour.

But then Zico decided to wake up from an apparent slumber by popping up on the back post to nod home an equaliser and it was back to square one for Milan. They dealt with the setback well, however, and before half-time midfield man Vinicio Verza swivelled well to drive a low shot past Fabio Brini in the Udinese goal. Few could argue the lead was not deserved.

The second half saw Oscar Damiani come closest to extending the Rossoneri's lead when he watched a shot ricochet off both posts before being cleared. At the other end, Massimo Mauro should have levelled but blasted over from a good position. It was a miss he would later regret.

With less than 10 minutes to play, Milan made what should have been the winning move. A header back across goal was met bravely by Blissett as he risked clattering into a goalpost. That should have been game, set and match for the boys in red and black.

But while they were a young side still looking for its identity, Udinese had some wily old professionals in their ranks. They might have been well shackled for much of the match but they suddenly came to life in the closing stages. Their collective quality was too much for Milan to handle.

It took something special to give Enzo Ferrari's men a lifeline. A neat one-two on the edge of the Milanese penalty area saw a ball chipped into the box in Zico's direction. The ball took a slight deflection off a home defender but the Brazilian adjusted brilliantly to swing an overhead kick past a helpless Ottorino Piotti. It was Zico's third two-goal game since arriving in Italy.

There were about three minutes to play when an improbable comeback was completed. Causio held off his marker on the right hand side of the penalty area and turned his man expertly before drilling a shot home. A little forward roll and leap in the air told you how much it meant to the former Juve man. The raincoat-sporting Castagner was raging on the sidelines.

"We made a few mistakes on all three goals," said a disconsolate Tassotti. "They are chronic errors, we have been making them since last year. People keep saying it is down to inexperience but maybe we will keep committing them as long as we live."

In truth, he need not have been quite so worried as he would go on to be part of one of the greatest defences Serie A has ever seen. However, that was some way in the future and Milan would finish eighth that year - not bad for a newly promoted side. Greater days were around the corner.

They would not, however, include coach Castagner. He had done a deal to move to city rivals Inter and was relieved of his post before the season came to an end. It did not work out well at the Nerazzurri for the ex-Perugia boss and he slowly slipped down the coaching ranks.

His opposite number, Ferrari, would also move on at the end of the campaign. He tried his luck in Spain, at Real Zaragoza, but like Castagner his managerial career was on the downward path. At least he had this fine display in Milan to look back on.

"I don't think anyone would have bet a lira on us at 3-1 down," admitted Causio after that game. "We got it to 3-2 straight away and then our character and experience came through. We showed our so-called 'attributes' and we managed to square the match."

"I feel good now," beamed Zico. "Plus Ferrari played me in a deeper role where I prefer to play and I have always played there in Brazil. But when I arrived in Udine they asked me to play a bit further forward."

Whatever position he was put in and no matter how many injuries he suffered, he certainly made an impact. A 19-goal haul saw him finish just behind Juve's Michel Platini in the Serie A goalscoring charts. It would be the peak of his time in Italy as he struggled for fitness the following year and managed just a handful of goals. But at least Udinese fans had the memory of an outstanding strike at the San Siro before letting him go back to Brazil.

Milan: Piotti; Tassotti, Evani (85 Spinosi); Icardi, Galli, Baresi; Carotti (65 Manzo), Battistini, Blissett, Verza, Damiani.

Udinese: Brini; Galparoli, Cattaneo; De Agostini, Edinho, Miano; Causio, Marchetti (78 Danelutti), Mauro (72 Pradella), Zico, Virdis.

Goals: 8 Baresi (pen), 40 & 84 Zico, 43 Verza, 81 Blissett, 87 Causio.

Fiorentina v Bologna

Stadio Artemio Franchi, 9 March 1997

There are some players who seem destined to play out their career in a superstar role while others spend their days in almost complete obscurity. But a third group enjoy a brief explosion of form which eclipses everything else they achieve before or after. Anselmo Robbiati was that kind of player.

The 1996/97 season was possibly his finest hour. In a midtable Fiorentina side he chipped in 11 goals over the course of the season - just one short of in-house legend Gabriel Omar Batistuta. Few of them were more perfectly executed or important than his strike against Bologna in a gripping encounter.

The Rossoblu were by far the better positioned side when their week 23 encounter rolled around in early March. They were in the hunt for European places while the Viola already seemed consigned to dour survival and little more. They were still no pushovers at the Artemio Franchi.

They went into the match tired but happy. In midweek they had recorded a historic 2-0 victory away to Benfica courtesy of goals from Batistuta and Francesco Baiano. It had put the Florentines in the driving seat in their Cup Winners' Cup quarter final.

For any seasoned Fiorentina follower, the Bologna match was a typical affair. The home side did its best to torment its fans for much of the game. The outcome was in the balance throughout the 90 minutes.

It was Bologna who took the lead when a Francesco Toldo error presented Kennet Andersson with an unexpected gift after just two minutes. He was only too happy to take it and give his team the lead. But it was a blow the Viola quickly recovered from.

Ciccio Baiano levelled matters from the penalty spot in the 19th minute - Batigol had been replaced as taker after a string of misses. But the home side slipped behind once again shortly afterwards, this time to a strike from Carlo Nervo that deflected off Aldo Firicano leaving Toldo stranded.

Claudio Ranieri brought his side into the dressing room at half time trailing 2-1. He took a gamble making all three changes at the interval replacing Sandro Cois, Rui Costa and Baiano with Giovanni Piacentini, Robbiati and Luis Oliveira respectively.

"There was nothing else I could do," explained the Fiorentina boss. "Those three had run out of gas and I could not wait any longer to replace them. We needed fresh legs and I couldn't worry too much about the balance of the team.

"I spoke to Rui on Saturday night and he told me he was tired. Playing against Benfica was a double exertion for him - both physically and emotionally - but he told me he wanted to play. Robbiati's not fully fit and can't play a whole game so I decided to give them a half each."

It proved to be a winning gamble but it would take two stunning free-kicks to turn the match on its head. The first was delivered by Batistuta - who else? - with such power and precision that even though Francesco Antonioli got a hand on it, it found the net. The second came from that man Robbiati.

In his perfect moment with a little more than 10 minutes to go he sized up his angles just right and swung the ball home. It was enough to get the Viola the win and send the Franchi crowd home with their nerves shredded as usual but ultimately happy. The man they called Spadino - after a character from the hit TV show Happy Days - deserved a big Fonzie thumbs up.

Bologna boss Renzo Ulivieri – regularly linked with the Fiorentina job – could not have been happy with the key role free-kicks played in his team's defeat but he decided to keep his counsel for once. "I'm going to behave myself in Florence," he said. "I've already paid a fortune in fines for my criticism of match officials. But it wasn't the usual Bologna – and if you don't play, you usually lose."

"We're back to winning ways and, above all, showing the old spirit," said Ranieri. "Now we have to keep on fighting without looking too much at the league table. I don't know if this can be a turning point for Fiorentina. Bologna's goals – for how they came about – were a couple of really hard blows to take. It wasn't easy to come back from that but the boys came out with pride and determination. We had been fighting without getting results for too long. All we can do now is carry on and play each game as if it were the last of the season."

The result made more difference to Bologna's season than it did to Fiorentina's. They slowly slipped out of the European places while the Tuscans remained mired in midtable. By the end of that campaign just four points, and a couple of places, separated them. It had not been a vintage year for either side.

But for the slimline Robbiati - who never managed to get much above 10 stone (64kg) throughout his career - it was one of his best seasons. About 40% of his total Fiorentina Serie A goals came in that magical 1996/97 campaign. He never scaled such heights again and shipped out to Napoli and then Inter where he failed to make much of an impact.

A return to Florence did not kick-start his career and he drifted down the leagues with Ancona, Grosseto, Monza, Como and Figline - alongside another old Viola hero Enrico Chiesa. He hung up his distinctive yellow boots a few years ago but his golden age will live forever in the minds of Fiorentina fans of a certain age. His star may not have shone for long, but when it did - like against Bologna - it surely shone brightly.

Fiorentina: Toldo; Carnasciali, Firicano, Falcone, Pusceddu; Kanchelskis, Cois (46 Piacentini), Rui Costa (46 Robbiati), Schwarz; Baiano (46 Oliveira), Batistuta.

Bologna: Antonioli; Tarozzi, Mangone, De Marchi, Paramatti; Brambilla, Marocchi, Scapolo (72 Cardone & 83 Bergamo), Nervo (57 Schenardi; Andersson, Kolyvanov.

Goals: 2 Andersson, 19 Baiano (rig), Firicano (og), 61 Batistuta, 78 Robbiati.

Inter v Sampdoria

Stadio Giuseppe Meazza, 9 January 2005

If you believe in leaving things late, there are probably few matches which would suit you better. Until the closing minutes of this game, Inter were dead and buried and the last rites long since administered. But in five amazing minutes, they somehow managed to produce a recovery which stunned even the most seasoned observer of Serie A.

The early stages of the game gave little hint at what was to come. The Nerazzurri peppered the visitors' goal with shots and former Milan youth product Francesco Antonioli had to look sharp to deny them. A comfortable home win looked far and away the most likely outcome.

But a hooked cross from Aimo Diana suddenly found the home defence a little bare. Max Tonetto had galloped clear at the far post and he drove a shot across Francesco Toldo and into the net. The visiting Doria faithful started to believe that a smash and grab triumph could be achieved. There was still, however, a long way to go.

The second half started in much the same way as the first had with Inter pressing hard and Samp having to defend resolutely. Time and again Antonioli was tested but a break from Francesco Flachi hinted that the Genoese side could still pose a threat. It was a signal which Roberto Mancini seemed to ignore as he took off Cristiano Zanetti to bring on Obafemi Martins to create an even more offensive formation. His opposite number, the expert Walter Novellino, responded by bringing on Vitali Kutuzov for the less mobile Fausto Rossini. It proved to be what looked like a matchwinning masterstroke.

In the 83rd minute another sweeping counter-attack doubled Samp's lead. Diana powered up the park and picked up a backheel-flick return pass from Flachi to gallop on towards goal. Another accurate cross found Kutuzov who thumped the ball into the roof of the net. His celebrations suggested he was pretty sure he had cemented a famous victory. "This game is locked up in the safe now," said the match commentator while Inter fans gathered up their banners in disgust and headed for the San Siro exits.

Anyone who left the ground missed seeing Mancini's substitutes finally have an effect. Alvaro Recoba, who had replaced Adriano before the game's second goal, fed Martins who produced a cool, outside-of-the-boot finish which felt like little more than consolation coming, as it did, in the 88th minute. The speed with which Inter retrieved the ball, however, showed they believed it was still possible to take something from the game.

They threw themselves at Samp like a storm force wind and, incredibly, a defence which had held firm for nearly an hour and a half was suddenly blown away. Some determined play from Martins saw him chase a lost cause and scoop the ball back across goal in injury time into the path of Bobo Vieri. The big hitman guided the ball home with his right foot and seemed to goad his own supporters for ever doubting they would get a result. The Doria players looked totally dejected.

That sinking feeling would only get more profound. Dejan Stankovic showed the presence of mind to roll a half-cleared header into the path of the advancing Recoba in the third minute of injury time and the Uruguayan did what he does best – put his left boot through the ball with a low drive which gave Antonioli no chance. He flapped his Inter shirt in celebration as if even he was a little bit astounded by the events which had just unfolded.

"He had 15 minutes to make an impact and he crammed in the match-winning goal, an assist and hit the post," swooned La Gazzetta dello Sport. "He was clearly in a hurry."

"There are games which can be a turning point for a player," said Mancini when asked about his matchwinner. "I hope this one can do that for Il Chino and he can start to show all the quality he has all the time. I have always said he has plenty of ability.

"We were 2-0 down but I don't really know how," continued Mancio. "We had created plenty and our defence was rarely troubled. It would have been incredible to lose this game. The boys were great but don't just talk about the character they showed because we played well before the comeback too."

"This game was a great advert for football and Inter in particular," crowed Inter President Massimo Moratti, before sniping at the fans who quit the ground early. "Anyone who left the stadium when Samp went 2-0 up made a mistake."

If there was elation among the Nerazzurri, there was understandable deflation in the Blucerchiati camp. A win which would have seen them take fourth place had ended up handing that position to their opponents. Their coach was understandably downhearted when he spoke to reporters.

"We played perfectly until Martins scored, then something incredible happened," said Novellino. "It was entirely our fault that we lost - we had the game already won. They only played for six minutes - unfortunately that was all they needed."

"Football doesn't always reward those who deserve it," he grumbled. "And today we deserved to win. They told me that this was the best Inter performance of the season which makes our display even more impressive. This is a fine Sampdoria side which leaves Milan."

The season, of course, would end up being a dark one for the Italian game with Juventus' Scudetto triumph cancelled from the record books as part of the Calciopoli verdicts. Inter would end up notionally in third place while Samp finished a creditable fifth as well. Both would be rewarded with European football which was the very least they deserved for dishing up one of the most incredible and enthralling fixtures ever witnessed in the Italian game.

Inter: Toldo; J Zanetti, Cordoba, Materazzi, Favalli; Emre (83 Karagounis), C Zanetti (64 Martins), Cambiasso, Stankovic; Adriano (77 Recoba), Vieri.

Sampdoria: Antonioli; C Zenoni, Castellini, Falcone (59 Pavan), Pisano; Diana, Palombo, Volpi, Tonetto; Flachi (90 Carrozzieri), Rossini (73 Kutuzov).

Goals: 44 Tonetto, 83 Kutuzov, 88 Martins, 91 Vieri, 93 Recoba.

Acknowledgements

Special thanks, as always, to my wife and children for giving me the time and space to produce this book. To all my followers on Twitter who joined in the nomination process for the 20th match of this edition and everyone who had nice things to say about the previous book. A nod to the archives of La Gazzetta dello Sport and La Stampa as well as the dedicated fans who stick video from many of these matches on the internet. A special mention to my cousin Marco and my old boss at Football Italia, John D Taylor, for ensuring the cover of this book was not just a blank page.

Also to everyone who has given me words of encouragement to keep writing when it might have been easier to give up the ghost. You know who you are and you know that your support has been vital fuel to keep me moving forward when it would have been easier to throw in the towel. If these fingers tap out any more words on the keyboard, it is down to all of you.

14369288R00043

Printed in Great Britain
by Amazon